Transition for Transformation

Transitioning churches into

relevant vehicles for

community transformation

Mike Holmes

Foreword

I was the Senior Pastor of Bethlehem Church Life Centre (BCLC) in South Wales from 1995 to 2012 and was part of a team leading it through significant change over several years. There was transition from a typical Welsh Pentecostal expression of church to a more culturally relevant missional congregation with a vision to see its community transformed.

This book is a remodelling of a case study I prepared as part of a master's degree documenting the process of the above transition and the changes that were required to achieve a workable vehicle for transforming the neighbourhood into a better expression of the kingdom of God.

After painting a picture of the church and its community at the beginning of this century, I include some detail of the market research we conducted in order to establish the need for the radical changes we eventually made. There is a brief discussion of the biblical mandate for the church's engagement with community transformation and the historical reasons why this has generally not been happening in recent times. I consider at length the process of transition we went through with reference to a number of relevant books.

The final chapter paints a picture of what the church looked like after transition with some insight as to its impact on community after six years of doing things differently.

It is not claimed that community transformation was achieved, but a process began with some encouraging signs.

It is hoped that this book will benefit others journeying through transition and provide practical principles that can be applied elsewhere.

Dedication and Acknowledgements

I would like to dedicate this book in memory of Lawrence Westcott, a core leader and life-long member of Bethlehem Church Life Centre, who died a premature death through cancer. Lawrence was a pioneer who saw something long ago of what BCLC became. He participated in drawing up initial plans for a new building but did not have the privilege of seeing those plans come to life. His faith, heart and encouragement were early foundations for the project described in these pages.

I would also like to acknowledge the role played by previous generations of members of BCLC; without their faith and commitment the church would not be there today.

Then there are those in more recent times who gave sacrificially of their finances and time to make a dream a reality. There are too many to mention, but you know who you are, and more importantly, so does God, who you have served so faithfully.

A special thank you to the late Mal Thomas, who God prepared for such a time as this. Mal's role in managing the building project and beyond was extraordinary.

Contents

Chapter 4

Transitioning the church...................................... 57

Chapter 5

Introduction

In many communities around the world there is a desperate requirement for a new approach to tackling needs and providing public services. The door of opportunity is wide open for local churches to place themselves at the heart of their community and provide solutions to the breadth of people's needs. Governments are beginning to recognise the local church as capable of making a distinct contribution in the public service field. Generally speaking, churches already make a huge contribution to the life of communities. According to an audit commissioned by the Welsh government, there is already one hundred million pounds worth of economic benefit provided by the Christian voluntary sector in Wales.[1] However, there is so much more that can be done by churches that have vision and motivation to do so, because like no other organization, they have a large volunteer work force that can quickly engage with community need.

This period of transition in the arena of public services demands that churches seize the moment to stand up and be counted among the key players in local community re-development. As Alan Roxburgh says, "The heart of the issue is: how can we be the church of Jesus in the midst of such continual, world-altering change?"[2]

---

[1] John M. Evans, *Faith in Wales: Counting for communities*, Cardiff: Gweini (2008), p9
[2] Alan Roxburgh, *The Sky is falling: Leaders lost in transition*, Eagle: Allelon Press (2006), p26

Bethlehem Church Life Centre (BCLC) aimed to empower people to fulfil their God given potential through loving and serving its community and surrounding area in practical ways. They believed that transforming their community into a better place to live was not only possible, but was their very reason to exist. They believed the church has got everything to do with community.

However, in order to transform community, transition of church must first take place. This book is a story of transition and will demonstrate key principles necessary for that challenging but rewarding story to develop.

As will be argued, community transformation reflects the heart of God; it is God's kingdom on earth. It is, therefore, not a new task but the very directive of the Lord Jesus Christ himself to his disciples[3] and forms part of Christ's model prayer he taught them[4]. "Mission is the task of God and we are called to cooperate with him".[5] However, in the post-modern society of the developed world, the values, vision and structures of many, if not most, congregations need to undergo a paradigm shift to avoid slipping further into obscurity. Various shifts have been part of Christian history, e.g. 'The Reformation', and have brought about significant change. We are overdue another. Many prominent church leaders see the need for major change in church

---

[3] Matthew 6:33, NKJV
[4] Matthew 6:10, NKJV
[5] TIM (Together in Mission) course notes, Module 406.1 *Mission History*, p6

practice. Beckham quotes Steve Covey in his book 'The Second Reformation':

> "*While a person may make small improvements by developing skills, quantum leaps in performance and revolutionary advances in technology require new maps, new paradigms, new ways of thinking about and seeing the world*".[6]

Rick Warren is looking for a second reformation. The first reformation, he says, was about beliefs, whereas the second one will be about behaviour, that is, what the church is doing.[7]

BCLC has gone through a paradigm shift. The church had been founded and operating in Pentecostal traditions for over seventy five years. It was predominantly inward looking, programme driven and event orientated. As will be argued later, it needed to become outward looking, purpose driven and process orientated. There needed to be a letting go of 'habits, values and patterns of actions... that known world that had shaped much of their life and provided its identity'. At the same time there needed to be a re-entering into the 'primary narratives and traditions of Christian life'.[8]

---

[6] William Beckham, *The Second Reformation*, Houston: Touch Outreach Ministries (1995), p18
[7] Rick Warren's Second Reformation. Interview with David Kuo. www.beliefnet.com (Dec 2009)
[8] TIM course notes, Module 406.3 *The Management and Culture of Change*, p30

The congregation radically transitioned over several years to become a culturally relevant missional congregation. I find this definition from Roxburgh and Romanuk helpful:

> *"A missional church is a community of God's people who live into the imagination that they are, by their very nature, God's missionary people living as a demonstration of what God plans to do in and for all of creation in Jesus Christ".*[9]

The vision of BCLC was cast, communicated and worked towards; its leadership widened, flattened and became more effective; its structures changed to facilitate an 'inside-out' approach. It's very 'DNA' changed. It did not just moved the deckchairs on the Titanic, it re-built the ship. It is from this practical, hands-on perspective that I write this book.

Changes to the leadership structure and how it functioned were profound over the time and I will place some emphasis on this area as I believe it to be a significant factor in our transition.

Churches need leaders who can give away rather than hold on to the power of office. Leaders who are thinking about tomorrow's church rather than yesterday's. Change requires much security and maturity in the leadership and even more so when the changes affect the leadership structures itself.

---

[9] Roxburgh & Romanuk, *The Missional Leader*, San Fransisco: Jossey-Bass (2006), pxv

The church became very different to what it was a few short years before. The changes were accelerated through the building of a new centre to house a multi-purpose community project. The centre housed a coffee shop, conference facilities, sport, health and fitness activities, various adult education courses as well as youth and children's work. It became a busy building open from 9am to 10pm five days a week.

It is my hope that this work will be of help to others who may be thinking of transitioning church in order to transform their communities.

Chapter 1

A Biblical mandate for community transformation

God's vision of society

One of the best definitions of community transformation I have come across is one by Vinay Samuel, who together with Chris Sugden edited the book, Mission as Transformation:

> *"Transformation is to enable God's vision of society to be actualized in all relationships, social, economic, and spiritual, so that God's will may be reflected in human society and his love be experienced by all communities, especially the poor."*[10]

The heart of God, as revealed through the Bible, is full of compassion, grace, mercy and love towards people. God is love, with the disposition of grace towards mankind. He describes himself as "The LORD, the LORD God, merciful and gracious, longsuffering, and abounding in goodness and truth, keeping mercy for thousands, forgiving iniquity and transgression and sin."[11]

---

[10] Samuel Vinay & Sugden Chris, *Mission as Transformation*, Oxford: Regnum Books (1999) inside front cover
[11] Exodus 34:6, NKJV

The apostle John puts it quite simply as "God is love."[12]

Probably the best known verse in the Bible summarises God's heart, "For God so loved the world that he gave his only begotten Son, that whoever believes in him should not perish but have everlasting life."[13]

There are approximately eight hundred Biblical references to God's justice and righteousness; many of these refer to looking after the orphan, the widow and the refugee. God makes it clear he is interested in those on the margins of society and wants his people to be instruments of healing, support and transformation.

When God is referring to his own glory in Exodus 33, he defines it as his goodness, grace and compassion,[14] that is, the practical out-workings of his love.

It is from this perspective that God looks upon the world of human beings.

The social conditions brought about by a tough economic climate together with the lifestyles of alcohol dependence, substance abuse, criminal activity and low morals have brought fracture and breakdown into our society resulting in deprivation and the fragmentation of our communities. The heart of God is for mankind to live together in a society which has righteousness and justice as its foundation with

---

[12] 1 John 4:16, NKJV
[13] John 3:16, NKJV
[14] Exodus 33:18-19, NKJV

mercy and compassion as its characteristics.

God cares deeply for the widow and the orphan, the hungry and the needy, the disabled and the disadvantaged, those who are oppressed and the foreigner. In fact the apostle James reminds his readers that "Pure and undefiled religion before God and the Father is this: to visit orphans and widows in their trouble, and to keep oneself unspotted from the world."[15]

When Jesus began his public ministry his message was simple: he had brought heaven with him.[16] He then proceeded to demonstrate and explain what that looks like. He demonstrated the loving rule and the grace-filled authority of God amongst people, healing, blessing and restoring them to God-given dignity and a new kingdom lifestyle. Simply put, Jesus brings God's vision for the world with him for all to see. Jesus didn't just talk about God's love in theory, but demonstrated God's love in action.

What has church got to do with community?

The most fundamental element for any congregation is to determine its nature and purpose. This is like the DNA of an organism. It is the essence, the ethos of the church, which is ingrained within it and determines what pours out from it. It is vital to get this right. It is like

---

[15] James 1:27, NKJV
[16] Mark 1:14-15, NKJV

the soil in which church members are nurtured. We may have an inspirational vision for what we would like these members to achieve, but without the right soil they will not grow appropriately. It is here that some congregations need their paradigm shift in order to grow. Their DNA is not missional as this statement indicates it should be: 'The church is the body of Christ on earth, engaged in His mission'.[17]

The Lambeth conference of 1988 defined mission as follows:

To proclaim the good news of the gospel

To teach, baptise and nurture new believers

To respond to human need by loving service

To seek to transform unjust structures of society

To strive to safeguard the integrity of creation, to sustain and renew the life of the earth.[18]

According to the Lambeth definition, a congregation engaged in mission will be impacting the world around them, transforming society through the five areas outlined above. Mission has a much more holistic dimension than proclamation evangelism. This integral mission approach enables all members of congregations to be empowered to serve and complete the good works God ordained for them to do by 'removing the walls' of the church that have restricted

---

[17] TIM course notes, Module 406.5 *From Vision to Reality*, p9
[18] TIM course notes, Module 406.5 *From Vision to Reality*, p9

many to traditional roles of service.

This is illustrated by Gibbs & Coffey in a list of common features of churches growing in England which shows an approach to evangelism centred on people and their needs.[19]

I enjoyed a two week tour of mission work in the North East area of Brazil in 2006. The churches I visited were all established through the work of one Mission organisation (Evangelical Action, Brazil). Each church has a mission minded approach to their activity. They call it 'integral mission'.[20] Their ethos is making a difference in their communities in many diverse, practical, relevant ways. There is proclamation and demonstration of God's unconditional love taking place. Martin Luther referred to 'Christians in earnest' as those 'who profess the gospel with hand and mouth'.[21]

Herrington, Bonnen & Furr refer to this as 'spiritual vitality' (loving God) and relational vitality (loving people) which they say not only empowers a local body of Christ, but also prepares a church to become God's instrument in the world.[22]

---

[19] Gibbs Eddie & Coffey Ian, *Church Next: Quantum Changes in Christian Ministry*, Nottingham: IVP (2000), p57.
[20] EAB website, www.eabrazil.com
[21] Beckham William, *The Second Reformation*, Houston: Touch Outreach Ministries (1995) Front Cover.
[22] Herrington Jim, Bonem Mike & Furr James, *Leading Congregational Change; Workbook: A practical Guide for the Transformational Journey*, Dallas: Jossy-Bass (2000), pp3-5

Therefore I define 'missional' as 'engagement with the world through proclamation and demonstration of God's love'.

Establishing this culture within the hearts of people is fundamental before any church transition can take place. People need to 'resonate' with any new world view, vision or values, before they will adopt new structures and strategies. When people feel good, they work at their best.[23]

Goleman observes:

> "Emotionally intelligent leaders know that their primal task is to look first to the organisational reality, identifying the issues with the full involvement of key individuals. They take the conversation to the organisation as a whole, using engaging processes to get people viscerally involved in unearthing the current reality, while tapping into individual and collective hopes for the future."[24]

It is, 'only to the degree that [the corporate vitality of pursuing God's vision] is achieved will church structures change in such a way as to empower its members for the kind of mission that 'cuts the ice' in the

---

[23] Goleman Daniel, Boyatziz Richard & McKee Annie, *The New Leaders: Transforming the Art of Leadership into the Science of Results*, Boston: Little Brown/Havard Business School Press (2002) p14

[24] Goleman Daniel, Boyatziz Richard & McKee Annie, *The New Leaders: Transforming the Art of Leadership into the Science of Results*, Boston: Little Brown/Havard Business School Press (2002) p210

contemporary world environment.'[25]

The holistic approach to mission once established in the hearts and minds of BCLC's congregation required new leadership and church structures.

BCLC's experience of engaging in integral mission in their community was both challenging and rewarding, leading to numerical church growth and many lives transformed. They had to move from a 'bless me' mindset, to a 'let me be a blessing'. For them this was the paradigm shift that Warren, Beckham, Wagner, Wheatley and McLaren refer to.

"Values are those deeply held, fundamental beliefs which consciously or unconsciously underpin and influence our behaviour."[26] BCLC believed their values expressed in single words and phrases reflected a missional DNA: God centred, people empowering, purpose driven, excellence, service, kingdom, love for God and people, integral mission, transformation, relevant, real, practical, no more boxes, inside-out church, fulfilling the 'great commission', the Bible – not a theory book to study but a manual for life, stretched faith, vibrant God present worship, growing spiritual giants, releasing people's potential and destiny, freedom in Christ, grace, commitment, team oriented leadership and church structure.

---

[25] TIM notes, Module 406.4 *Mission and Empowerment*, p11
[26] TIM notes, Module 406.5 *From Vision to Reality*, p13

They endeavoured to communicate these values to everyone in the church. It is important to ensure that all members understand a church's values and priorities so that they know the value of their own contribution and how it impacts missional outcomes.[27]

Having a deep understanding across the organisation of the essential nature and purpose of the church is the first step in the process of developing a vision strategy. It may take some time as the very DNA of a congregation is unravelled and then reformed. Wheatley writes that despite the lack of objective reality in the world:

> *"There is an essential role for organisational intent and identity. Without a clear sense of who they are, and what they are trying to accomplish, organisations get tossed and turned by shifts in their environment. No person or organisation can be an effective co-creator with its environment without clarity about who it is intending to become".[28]*

In terms of the process of developing a vision strategy, the first questions to be asked are, 'What kind of church are we and what are we to do?'[29] Out of the answer to these questions should arise a

[27] TIM course notes, Module 406.5 *From Vision to Reality*, p22
[28] Margaret Wheatley, *Leadership and the New Science*, San Fransisco: Berret-Koehler (2006), pp38,39
[29] Aubrey Malphurs, *Advanced Strategic Planning Method*, www.malphursgroup.com (Dec. 2009)

complaint, i.e. a dissatisfaction of the status quo and the need for the paradigm shift resulting in a fresh discovery of the church's nature and mission. The next questions are, 'Who are we and why do we do what we do?' This is where we discover the passionate, biblical core beliefs or values.[30]

The processes of determining purpose and vision are similar and we will discuss this aspect later. In fact, clear vision may be the catalyst to changing the DNA of the church.

Congregations that adopt a focussed approach in demonstrating and proclaiming God's heart of love for people will not only have a transformational vision, but also God's vision, with the likely outcome that the number of people living under the kind and loving canopy of God's kingdom will increase.

Transformational vision will see things from heaven's point of view. When a congregation lives from the perspective of God's love for people, it understands that it is called to be a carrier of this love into its city and streets: touching individual lives with grace, healing, compassion and acts of kindness that make a difference. Isaiah 58 encourages this practical engagement with community by exhorting God's people to come to the aid of those who are oppressed and burdened, share food with the hungry, provide shelter for the

---

[30] Aubrey Malphurs, *Advanced Strategic Planning Method*, www.malphursgroup.com (Dec. 2009)

homeless, donate clothing for the needy, to repair the foundations and restore community (see Isaiah 58:6-10). This will involve congregations providing the care, stability, discipline and role models of family life to a generation substantially deprived of a loving environment in which to grow; recovering the ground of social involvement and integration (Dan Boucher in his e-book "Taking our place" describes how the church initiated many of our great social institutions in areas such as education, health and family); becoming a leader within its community, taking responsibility for its community; becoming a pacesetter, forerunner and innovator, an influencer for good. As we begin to do this we become increasingly aware that Jesus is already at work in people's lives awaiting our involvement.

Such vision is important in inspiring the kind of action necessary for community transformation.

Why churches do not engage with community

In the Western developed world there has been a dualism between congregational evangelism and social action for various historical reasons outlined below. This dualism has unconsciously shaped the worldview of many Christians keeping us from communicating Christ in word *and* deed.

The holistic or integral purpose of the church to love the Lord with all our heart, soul, and mind *and* love our neighbour as ourselves[31] has been neglected. Congregations tend to either emphasize evangelism or social action or pursue incomplete versions of both.

> *"This dualism has led to specialized languages for each that tend to sharpen the divide between rather than integrate the two aspects of the Christian mandate to the detriment of each, for we know we cannot be effective at social action without deep evangelistic spiritual transformation, and our evangelism is often weak and incomplete without visible, tangible, and practical evidence of our love for our neighbours and the world outside our church congregation."[32]*

What are the historical reasons why churches do not fully engage in community?

Historical Christianity in the 19th Century would suggest that it was normal for churches to be fully engaged with the society around them. Kathleen Heasman, estimates that 75% of UK voluntary organizations in the second half of the 19th Century had an evangelical ethos.[33]

Spurgeon and Barnardo homes, the YMCA, Sunday Schools, day schools, the temperance movement and many educational and cultural

---

[31] Matthew 22:38-40, NKJV.

[32] Dr Peter Clarke. *Understanding an integral mission approach*. www.viva.org (Jan. 2007)

[33] Cited by Boucher Daniel, *Taking our place. Church in the community*, Cardiff: Gweini (2002), p3

projects would be examples of such organisations. Many of these projects helped people to read and understand morality as well as the gospel. The temperance society set up alternatives to the public houses such as coffee taverns, literary societies and workman's libraries. It also put its energies into political campaigning and brought about the 1881 Sunday closing Act in Wales. The work of chapels in regard to adult education at that time was extraordinary.

It should be noted at this point that by the end of the 19th Century many evangelicals were bemoaning the loss of 'spiritual life' to undergird this activism and regretted the fact that activism had become an end in itself. In fact, church decline set in at this time. This, perhaps, should warn us of the importance of holding activism in balance with the other important roles churches have.

What issues could have reversed the social activity in the 19th Century to the more individual orientated Christianity that is prevalent today?

John Stott identifies five key factors. Firstly, the rise of liberal theology, leaving evangelicals needing to devote more time to preaching scriptural truth. Secondly, the development of the social gospel movement where liberal theologians took hold of social issues and sought to bring in the kingdom of God without God's help through social action alone. This led to further distancing of evangelicals from a social agenda.

Thirdly World War 1 produced much cynicism amongst many

evangelicals who believed humanity was so evil, the only way forward was to develop their own individual relationship with God and look for the second coming of Christ. Fourthly there was an eschatological factor, a form of pre-millennialism developed that preached that the world would become worse and worse before the return of Christ and that by engaging in social action and thus improving the world, would effectively slow down the return of Christ. Finally middle class conservatism led to unsympathetic or indifferent attitudes to the poor and marginalized. [34]

I have come across all five factors in recent years that still hold some Christians back from social engagement today. There could also be other significant national factors.

For example, in Wales, the 1904 Revival also had an impact on all of this. Initially it transformed society, but then moved into a holiness movement and withdrawal from engagement with national life and such things as the arts, sport and politics. Fifty years ago at BCLC, sport was considered 'worldly' and people where forbidden to get involved with it. Generally speaking, evangelicals withdrew from society and proclaimed the gospel just through the spoken word.

There were also political changes that impacted the churches

---

[34] John Stott, *New Issues Facing Christians Today*, Grand Rapids: Zondervan (1999), pp8-11

involvement in community. A series of Acts of Parliament[35] reduced the voluntary sectors involvement in society as the State gradually took over responsibility for social issues.

I would maintain that the church of the 20th century mistakenly surrendered social involvement to the government of the day and retreated into its own sub-culture, becoming increasingly irrelevant to society. I believe that God's current word to the church is to recover this ground and become a force for good within the community.

There is currently a political will to engage the voluntary sector more. It started with contracting out into the private sector some of the public sector activities, but has now developed with more opportunity for partnerships with local government and national government departments. This was the experience of BCLC as they rediscovered the Biblical mandate for social engagement and started networking with governmental bodies.

In this chapter we have considered the Biblical and indeed historical mandate for the church engaging with community to help bring about a transformation which reflects the kingdom of God. In the next chapter we will look at the local context of BCLC to show the background of the church and its community.

---

[35] The Pensions Act 1908; The National Insurance Act 1911; The National Health Service Act 1946; The National Insurance Act 1946; The National Assistance Act 1948; The Voluntary Sector post 1951

Chapter 2

Church and community background

A brief history of Bethlehem Church Life Centre (BCLC)

The founding members of BCLC were people converted to Christianity through the well documented 'Welsh Revival' of 1904, when an estimated 100,000 people across Wales were swept into the chapels in the space of a few months. During the early 1920's several of these people living in Cefn Cribwr began to meet together in a cottage. The numbers gathering gradually grew and by the end of the decade there was a need for a permanent place of worship. A plot of land was purchased and the first building, named Bethlehem Pentecost Church, was constructed in 1932. The name was chosen to reflect the vision of that time to be a 'house of bread' and continue to develop the use of the spiritual gifts that had re-emerged during the revival.

The congregation continued to enlarge by those joining it locally as well as being swelled by others returning to Wales after having been away to work during the thirties. By the early 1950s the building was full to capacity, and so in 1952 it was demolished and another building was erected. This building has been extended in various ways over the last 60 years and from it the church has sought to be relevant to the changing community around it. BCLC's ability to adapt to contemporary society without losing the timeless values with which it started, is perhaps why it has flourished in a decreasing market-place.

This brief history indicates that BCLC was well established and has had a presence in the community for around a hundred years. Its influence on the community over the years was highlighted in 2000, when over a hundred visitors attended an exhibition of photographs and memorabilia in the church, and a new edition of the church's history, entitled 'The Revival's Children', was published to celebrate its 70th anniversary.

Before the construction of the new building in 2005, the buildings consisted of a front foyer with two toilets, giving access to the main hall with a comfortable seating capacity of one hundred and fifty, a two story extension built in the 1970's (housing offices, toilets and a room dedicated for prayer) at the rear, and a further extension (a more general use hall with small kitchen area) built in 1996 on the rear east side of the property. There was also a small car-park area on the east side of the main hall.

A typical week's programme of building use at that time would have been as follows:

  Office used each day.

Sunday:

Morning: All rooms used for church service and Sunday School

Classes.

Evening: Most rooms used for church service and youth activities.

Monday:

Evening: All rooms used for children's activities followed by youth activities.

Tuesday:

Evening: 'Prayer Tower' used for church activities

Wednesday:

pm : Main Hall used for Senior Citizen's activities

Thursday:

Morning: Small hall used for Parent & Toddler group

Friday:

Evening: 'Prayer Tower' used for church activities.

The style of most BCLC meetings at the end of the previous century was of a Pentecostal or Charismatic nature. There was wide and open use of the gifts of the Spirit by members of the congregation during contemporary worship and Biblical preaching to the converted.

At this time it was rare to have un-churched visitors at meetings and even rarer to see people saved. Alpha courses were run from time to time but it was difficult to populate them because the congregation had exhausted the pool of potential invitees. Other evangelistic events were arranged but with little response.

The church largely maintained a stability of numbers (approximately seventy), by replacing those who left or died with others who chose to transfer from other churches or Christians who moved into the area.

As a result of a fierce storm in the late 1990's, the asbestos roof of the building was damaged. It was temporarily repaired, but a new roof was needed. This generated discussion and prayer as to what the next step should be, and it was eventually decided to take the opportunity to rebuild the property rather than make repairs to what was an ageing building.

A Picture of the Community of Cefn Cribwr

The village of Cefn Cribwr has a population of approximately 1500. The geographical position of the village is unusual in that it is built on a long ridge of almost 2 miles in length between the villages of Aberkenfig to the east and Kenfig Hill to the west. Five miles to the south-east lies the town of Bridgend and the Vale of Glamorgan. Because its buildings are spread over the length of the ridge, it is by no means an ideal village layout. To some, it is a mirror image of a typical Welsh Valley village (a valley village on the top of a mountain). The spirit of the typical Welsh valley communities certainly exist in Cefn

Cribwr. Most people are known to each other, a change in someone's personal circumstances travels fast and people will rally around a need.

Cefn Cribwr is situated in the County Borough of Bridgend. Welsh Government's statistics placed the village in the lower end of the All Wales Index of Multiple Deprivation, being 340th of 865, with education, health and employment featuring even lower at 154th, 224th and 323rd respectively; these are all below the Welsh national average.[36]

The village community hall (Miners Welfare Hall) of corrugated iron construction, was opened in 1924 by Mr. Stanley Baldwin, the first Labour Prime Minister. Its position in the centre of the village is advantageous but with no parking facilities and being within a few feet of a busy road is limited in its ability to fulfil a truly multi-purpose function for the 21st Century.

The playing field facilities provided by Bridgend CBC are situated on the east side of the village. A large car parking area is provided on the east side of the playing fields next to BCLC.

The main organisations in the community were six churches, the

---

[36] *Welsh Index of Multiple Deprivation 2005: Local Authority Analysis – Bridgend,* www.wales.gov.uk

Rugby Club, the Bowls Club, the British Legion Club, three Public Houses, the Community Association (which runs the community hall), the local Labour Party and the Primary School. Most of these organisations have their own facilities or hire the facilities of the other village organisations.

The decision to rebuild BCLC was followed by another decision which proved to be pivotal to the future of BCLC. The decision was made to construct a building for the community as well as for the church's own use. This decision dovetailed with the need for a multi-purpose building in the village with a variety of facilities, which would meet some of the needs of a modern village community and its various organisations and have adequate car parking arrangements. To be situated near to the centre of the village and to the playing fields, would also be advantageous.

Listening to God.

It is important to point out that the decisions outlined above were not made without listening to God.

The Psalmist talks about the gods of the heathen as having, "ears but they do not hear"[37]   Christians are in danger of having the same ailment when it comes to hearing God. God is speaking all the time in

---

[37] Psalm 115:6, KJV

various ways; many hear but fail to listen. What is God saying to the individual, to the church and to the world? Listening to what God is doing; listening to his heartbeat is a missional requirement. I believe BCLC's experience of God's favour was the result of hearing his heart for community transformation and taking the appropriate steps towards that vision.

If we are to make a difference as Christians in our world, we need to hear God. Joyce Hugget in her book, 'Listening to God', quotes Russian born Catherine de Hueck Doherty:

> *'If we are to witness to Christ in today's market places, where there are constant demands on our whole person, we need silence. If we are to be always available, not only physically, but by empathy, sympathy, friendship, understanding and boundless caritas, we need silence. To be able to give joyous, unflagging hospitality, not only of house and food, but of mind, heart, body and soul, we need silence'[38]*

In order to listen to others we first need to have listened to God in the place of silence. Listening to God should be our starting place before turning our ear to others. Prayer in a variety of forms became a key factor in BCLC's journey.

---

[38] Quoted in J. Huggett, *Listening to God*, London: Hodder & Stroughton (1986), p35

In 1999 a small group of Indonesians representing a mega-church based in Jakarta visited BCLC. It was suggested that the upper room upstairs in the rear of the building could be used as a 'Prayer Tower'. This room has a commanding view across the Vale of Glamorgan towards Cardiff, South over the Bristol Channel and West towards Swansea. It was decided to convert this room into a place of prayer for the nations. Various national flags were collected together with maps and the room was refurbished and decorated with these collections. Visitors came to pray from many parts of the world for revival and some notable meetings took place. The room was even featured on a BBC television programme in the height of the foot and mouth outbreak of 2001 where I was filmed praying that the local farmers of our region would be spared the disease.

Prayer continued in this room until work on the new building commenced in 2004. In the middle of the night during one of the eight hour prayer meetings that were held every month for seven years, the people assembled were singing a song which requested God to 'heal the land'. During this song I realised that the frequent requests for God to send revival were not right because we were asking God to do things that he wanted us to do. We were effectively praying for God to play our part in the transformation of society. This revelation was a turning point for BCLC. Instead of talking about revival, which tends to imply a supernatural move of God which convicts people of their need for him and sweeps them into churches, the church started talking of transformation which provides scope for humans to play their part beyond prayer.

This chapter has painted the background of BCLC and the community. The next chapter adds to the picture by describing the research undertaken to establish the need for a community building so that the steering group could determine the design of the new centre and apply for external funding.

Chapter 3

Market research – establishing the need for a community building

Community Exegesis

There is a commonly used truism that says, 'Those who fail to plan, plan to fail'. Before vision can be fully developed, much ground work needs to be done to gather information relevant to the mission. This information will become foundational for what is to be built. As Wheatley says, 'We must interact with the world in order to see what we might create".[39] However, such 'environmental scans', as Malphur terms it, need to be done regularly, given the shifting nature of the environment and the very impact subsequent mission may have.

> *'If our churches want to relate to and reach our culture, they must spend time exegeting the culture as well as the Bible. In short, they must be culture watchers…*
>
> *When the church exegetes the general environment, not only does it seek to discover what is taking place now, but it is looking for future trends or major shaping forces in five generic environments that will affect its future. They are the social, technological, economic, political, and philosophical*

---

[39] Margaret Wheatley, *Leadership and the New Science*, San Fransisco: Berret-Koehler (2006), p38

environments'.[40]

BCLC did not set out initially to intentionally listen to these five specific environments. The main aim was to discover the general needs within the community. However, the church found that listening to future trends in all five environments enabled it to secure funding for subsequent projects that government departments were prioritising.

Various methods of research and sources of information can be explored. In BCLC's case, they conducted surveys to assess the felt needs of the community, researched census and government statistics, conversed with community leaders, profiled the community, capitalised on local knowledge and past experience and observed the trends in Government thinking. They also surveyed the members of the congregation to produce a gift and skill database. They took a 'process centring' perspective which required starting with the 'customers' and what they wanted and working backwards from there.[41]

Strategies were also needed to provide a sustainable model for the long-term. For example, when trying to alleviate poverty, it is ineffective to simply deal with the social issues without also

---

[40] Aubrey Malphurs, *Planting Growing churches*, Grand Rapids: Baker Books (1998), p118

[41] Michael Hammer, *Beyond Reengineering*, New York: Harper Collins (1996), p9

generating business and employment opportunities. All this information was documented into a business plan for potential funders to study. If the feasibility of mission projects is robust enough to attract external, even secular funding, then this is a positive indication that they have the potential to succeed.

Kotter remarks, 'Feasibility means that a vision is grounded in a clear and rational understanding of the organisation, its market environment and competitive trends'.[42]

One of the purposes of this book is to provide guidance to others who may be embarking on similar transformational projects. This chapter deals in length with the preparatory work required to establish projects relevant for an area. This market research is obligatory if any external funding is to be obtained, as it will form the basis for a required business plan. Even if such funding is not applied for, careful exegesis of the community is sensible to establish the most effective and worthwhile projects.

Conducting such research, compiling business plans and applying for external funding was part of the church's transition. These practices forced it to carefully look at its community needs in ways it had not done before and to question its attitude to outside funding. Through debate and reflection BCLC changed its corporate view on pursuing

---

[42] John P. Kotter, *Leading Change*, Boston: HBS Press (1996), p75

the funding necessary for the project. If it had not travelled down this road of new thought, it is unlikely this book would have ever been written!

Listening to communities and culture.

In the parable of the Good Samaritan, Jesus talked about two people who failed to respond to the cries of an injured man and one who did. All three people walking down that road that day heard the same cries for help. Only one listened. The Good Samaritan then helped the man.[43] There are many cries for help in our communities that are being heard every day, but few are really listening. In order to be effective in mission, we need to have ears that are open to the anxieties and needs of community, for example, what does the gospel have to say about such things as image, money or violence?

Becoming relevant to community begins by listening to it. BCLC sought to transform community, to make their area a better place to live. Before embarking on a plan of action to fulfil this vision, it listened to the community through the research methods detailed below. It endeavoured to remove its own filters on society and look at what was really there.

The major research tools that were used to establish the need of the project were:

---

[43] Luke 10:30-37, NKJV

A community survey

The 2001 Census Information

The All Wales index of multiple deprivation (already referenced in the previous chapter)

The Bridgend County Borough Councils 15 year strategy document. 'Communities that Care' project report, resource audit and action plan.

Community Survey

A live door to door community survey was completed in 2002 and the results are summarized below.

There were three basic questions asked by interview:

1. How important do you think it is to have a community building that can provide amenities for young people in Cefn Cribwr?

2. What amenities do you think would be appropriate in such a building? This question was accompanied by nine options.

3. Would you use such facilities if they were available to you?

The total number of people interviewed was 128. This represented nearly 20% of the 665 households in Cefn Cribwr. None of these people were regular attendees of BCLC.

Age range breakdown:

11-25 years: 27%

26-60 years: 46%

60+ years: 27%

Results of the survey (percentage of the 128 people who responded)

1. How important do you think it is to have a community building that can provide amenities for young people in Cefn Cribwr?

Very Important: 88%

Important: 12%

Moderately Important: 0%

Not Important: 0%

Those interviewed were encouraged to also make comments related to the questions. For this question, individuals believed that a new community building could provide young people with the support, encouragement and motivation they need to help them grow into valuable adults and achieve their potential. They felt there was nothing locally for young people and that a building would keep them off the streets and reduce vandalism. Some living close by were worried about policing the young people who would use the building, but were agreeable as long as any extra noise was curtailed at night.

2. What amenities do you think would be appropriate in such a building?

Adult/youth education sure: 8%	Yes: 83%	No: 9%	Possibly/not
Children/youth clubs sure: 1%	Yes: 99%	No: 0%	Possibly/not
Computer facilities sure: 2%	Yes: 93%	No: 5%	Possibly/not
'Drop in' area sure: 6%	Yes: 91%	No: 3%	Possibly/not
Indoor games sure: 1%	Yes: 98%	No: 1%	Possibly/not
Indoor training/exercise sure: 4%	Yes: 96%	No: 0%	Possibly/not
Meeting/conference facilities sure: 6%	Yes: 85%	No: 9%	Possibly/not
Parent & Toddler group Possibly/not sure: 2%	Yes: 93%	No: 5%	
Sports Possibly/not sure: 0%	Yes: 100%	No: 0%	

For this question, individuals comments showed they were enthusiastic about all the amenities suggested and could see that the facilities would benefit the whole community not just young people.

Some suggested other uses of the building such as wedding receptions, a coffee shop, evening classes, skateboard facilities and providing activities during summer holidays. Apart from skateboarding, BCLC adopted all these suggestions.

3. *Would you use such facilities if they were available to you?*

Yes: 85%

No: 10%

Possibly/not sure: 5%

Individuals felt the facilities would be good for the whole family and enable them to learn new skills. They thought a new centre would be a place to relax and meet others and they would definitely use it. Others thought they would not have enough time to use the facilities or they lived too far away or were too old. However, even those who did not think they would use the facilities themselves felt the project would be a great success and looked forward to seeing it completed.

As can be seen from these results, the general support for the project in the village was overwhelmingly positive from all age groups. Out of all the homes visited only two people felt the project unnecessary, but they were not prepared to complete a survey form and have their opinion documented. Of the 15% of those surveyed who either said no or were unsure as to whether they would use the facilities, 58% of these were 61+ with the remaining 42% 41+. However, the majority of senior citizens (63%) and the majority of those 41+ (60%) could see value for themselves, through keep fit, adult education or 'drop-in' amenities.

All of the amenities that were listed on the survey were popular. Nearly all the 'no's' and the 'not sures' in this section were from young people aged 11-16 surveyed, who perhaps did not understand or were unable to see a direct value to themselves of certain amenities.

Various comments from the survey have been précised above; there follows one more from a respected and long standing resident:

> *"I think provision for our young people is the most important single social issue confronting us in Cefn, and there is little sign that anybody but the sporting organisations (in their own way) and yourselves are addressing the issue."* [44]

'Communities that Care' project report, resource audit and action plan.

From 2000 to 2002 BCLC was involved in the Rowntree Foundation's 'Communities that Care' initiative, sitting on the governing body's

---

[44] Neville Granville (retired teacher, local historian and author)

discussions on the problems of youth in our area.[45] BCLC and its work were mentioned in the local report that was produced.[46]

This report expressed the need for increased facilities for young people, to integrate and be involved in community and to reduce the risk of aimless loitering, drug abuse and disruptive behaviour. BCLC believed that their project fitted in with these aspirations to provide the kind of facilities that youth will use and where they feel they are welcomed and part of what is happening in the community.

The CtC report and action plan, which built on the analysis of a survey carried out amongst over 600 young people between the ages of 11 and 16 in the Cefn Cribwr, Kenfig Hill, Pyle and Corneli district, highlighted the domains of risk that were significant in the area and are detailed in the table below.

Domain	Risk
School	Low school achievement identified first in primary schools
Community	Community disorganisation and neglect

---

[45] Iain Crow, Alan France, Sue Hacking, and Mary Hart *Does Communities that Care work? An evaluation of a community-based risk prevention programme in three neighbourhoods,* York: Joseph Rowntree Foundation (2004)
[46] Much of this local report was published in the Rowntree Foundation document of the previous reference. I have referenced data from the unpublished local report.

Community	Availability of drugs including alcohol
Family and Individuals	Condoning problem behaviour
Friends and peers	Condoning problem behaviour

The Resource Audit carried out by CtC identified a variety of youth work available to the young people of the district, which needed to be supported and sustained, as well as barriers or gaps in the current provision.

Census and IMD information

The 2001 census information reflected the Index of Multiple Deprivation referenced in the previous chapter in the Community Background section. The statistics showed that Cefn Cribwr had a more unhealthy population that the average of England and Wales. For example, 14.7% of the population of the village described their health as 'not good' and 25.7% said they had a 'limiting long-term illness' compared to 9.2% and 18.2% respectively for England and Wales.

The Bridgend 15 year Community Strategy.

Much of this chapter describes the processes needed to gather appropriate data for a business plan. These processes may seem far removed from usual Christian practice. However, it is worth mentioning at this point, that God was not removed from the process. God was evident within every step taken on this unusual journey. There were many confirmations from God along the way that he was favouring BCLC, such as the miraculous provision for the project that I will refer to later.

Another confirmation was the publishing of Bridgend County Borough Council's fifteen year community strategy. This was very similar to BCLC's own vision statement that had been formed just days before. I will expand on BCLC's vision later, but the leadership realised that BCBC's strategy reflected much of the church's in terms of community transformation.

The overarching Aims of the Strategy as stated by BCBC:

1. To **improve the quality of life for all** – to create a place where everyone can enjoy living, working and relaxing, and live life to the full.

2. To **look after our environment** through a more sustainable pattern of development.

3. To increase **prosperity**, by investing in lifelong learning, improving skills and supporting new business.

4. To have **safer communities** where crime levels decline and fear of crime is tackled so that all local people feel safe and secure.

5. To achieve a **healthier** county borough, by tackling health inequalities and promoting healthy lifestyles.

6. To have a more **inclusive** county borough where everyone is supported to maximise their potential and live a full life.

This gave the leadership more confidence to pursue a transformational agenda in partnership with secular authorities. If we understand the kingdom in the terms described in chapter one, then Local Government could be said to have a kingdom agenda, as does the church, but it is the church that can provide the missing spiritual dimension.

Growing political support for faith group projects

The worth and value of faith communities in our society has been recognised by Government and by the Charities Commission. The consultation document 'Private Action, Public Benefit' published by the Cabinet Office in September 2002 recognised the important role that churches and other private charitable organisations play in the life of communities.

The following are some quotes from December 2002 supporting

projects like BCLC's:

> *"We should use the skills and capacity that faith communities*
> *have, that great energy, and ensure that they are used*
> *appropriately for those who would welcome access to them...*
> *Their faith informs their mission. We should accept that and*
> *recognise that that can be funded by central grants and by*
> *the Charity Commission with appropriate safeguards... We*
> *need to revisit the positive contributions made by the whole*
> *range of faith communities in Wales and in Britain."[47]*

> *"The Assembly Government of Wales is not in a position to*
> *revive our historic faith. It can however make sure that it*
> *does not put roadblocks in the way of faith inspired*
> *community initiatives. And it can recognise that while the*
> *political life of a nation together is important, the roots of a*
> *culture tap deep not just into our history and our traditions*
> *but into those ultimate and fundamental beliefs of which*
> *religion is the source."[48]*

Responding to the contention that Christians should focus exclusively on developing their personal inward relationship with God, and not get distracted by social and political activity, Janet Ryder stated:

---

[47] David Melding AM, 17th December 2002, The National Assembly for Wales.
[48] Lord Griffiths of Fforestfach, 9th December 2002, IWP Lecture, Aberystwyth.

"Look at what the Bible says. Those who think we can respond adequately through academic bible study have not understood the message. We can't keep ourselves apart. For me Jesus never did. He engaged and so must we."[49]

The developing aims of the project.

The market research outlined above helped BCLC formulate the overall aims of the project as it understood them at the time. They were:

To provide appropriate accommodation and facilities for a growing youth work within the community.

To provide a village community facility suitable for today's modern requirements.

To begin to tackle some of the problems highlighted in the 'Communities that Care' project report, resource audit and action plan.

To provide facilities to improve the general health of the community.

To provide the members of BCLC with increased capacity to fulfil their mission to the community, region and beyond.

To provide the necessary infrastructure to enable BCLC to

[49] Janet Ryder AM, for a Cardiff Institute for Contemporary Christianity (CICC) politics interview in 2003.

achieve its goals.

The current BCLC buildings at that time could not adequately provide for the range and number of children and youth making use of the facilities. The aim was to make provision for a range of activities reflecting the perceived needs that were highlighted by the market research. The existing main hall had a very limited scope for use, being designed as a main meeting and worship room, although it had been used to a limited extent for children's work for over 20 years.

The new hall would be of sufficient size to accommodate a full size basketball court and other courts such as five-a-side soccer, badminton or short court tennis, thereby providing a health benefit facility for the expanding youth work. BCLC would seek to fulfil the 2007 Youth Work Curriculum Statement for Wales which states:

> 'the purpose of youth work is to promote equality of opportunity for all young people in order that they may fulfil their potential as empowered individuals and as members of groups and communities; and to support young people to develop attitudes and skills which enable them to make purposeful use of their personal resources and time'.[50]

---

[50]

www.cwvys.org.uk/en/docs/Youth_Work_Curriculum_Statement_for_Wales_English.pdf (Dec 2009)

This would mean that BCLC's youth work should offer opportunities which are educative, participative, empowering, and expressive.

The new facilities would also benefit BCLC's evolving vision to see the community transformed by being better equipped to serve people.

The members and friends of the church fully supported the project and agreed with the aims and purposes that it sought to achieve. This was demonstrated in the way they generously worked and gave to the activities organised to raise money for the project. For example, during the summer of 2002 more than two hundred and fifty donors sponsored a cycle ride and raised more than £1,500.

More than £150,000 was eventually raised towards the project. This money came mainly from local people. Some substantial sums of up to £2,500 have also been given by friends and supporters outside of the area and some from as far away as Australia, Indonesia and America.

As more focused thought went into the building design it was decided to make the rooms as multi-purpose as possible in order to provide maximum sustainability for the project's economic success. It would be suitable for a variety of recreational and sporting activities as well as large meeting or conference use. Smaller rooms would accommodate other activities such as education, I.T. or as small meeting rooms.

Improved storage and kitchen facilities at the rear would allow use of the facility for functions and conferences.

From the analysis of the survey, the other market research tools, and knowledge of the limited community facilities in Cefn for youth activities, functions, and conferences, the list of proposed and possible uses for the new centre were:

Sport, Recreation, Exercise & Training, Sports Training, Keep Fit, Drama, Music, Conferences, Education, Computer and IT Courses, Adult Education, Functions,

Youth Drop-in Centre, Adult Drop-in and Advice Centre, Training Courses, Local Schools Educational & Recreational Use, Meetings (large & small).

The Centre would be available for use by local sporting clubs and other organisations as there are no indoor facilities of this nature in the village. The local primary school also expressed an interest in using the facility.

There were no other similar facilities or projects planned for the village of Cefn Cribwr or within a five mile radius.

Cefn Cribwr is central to South Wales with good road and rail networks locally. BCLC also had use of the adjacent public car park with parking spaces for up to eighty cars.

The adjacent Bridgend CBC playing field facilities enhanced the value of the project. They complemented each other.

I have described in this chapter the research that was undertaken to establish the need within the local area for a new building providing relevant facilities that would contribute to the transforming of the community.

We now need to turn our attention to the process of transitioning the church towards community transformation. I see this next chapter as the most important in this book and have therefore devoted the most pages to it.

Chapter 4

Transitioning the church

Change or die

Margaret Wheatley, in her book, Leadership and the New Science, tells a story of the famous physicists Neils Bohr and Werner Heisenburg. In the early twentieth century, they faced a situation analogous in many ways to ours; their theories did not fit their newest data. From this frustration, as the Old Newtonian paradigm proved inadequate to cope with subatomic reality, a breakthrough occurred and quantum theory was born.[51]

Brian McLaren in his thought provoking book, 'The Church on the other side', regards maximising discontinuity as a first strategy in the quest for organisational change that will enable churches to become and remain relevant.

He writes:

> "the degree of change we are experiencing now is such that small measures (of change), even a lot of them, are not enough. Instead, we need major change, qualitative change, revolution, rebirth, reinvention, and not just once, but

---

[51] Margaret Wheatley, *Leadership and the New Science*, San Fransisco: Berret-Koehler (2006), pp5-6

repeatedly for the foreseeable future."[52]

BCLC went through a revolution over an eight year period to become a missional congregation. During the last five years of that revolution, church attendance grew by over 300%. (This included many whose lives were transformed and came to faith, others who transferred from other churches preferring BCLC's vision and still others who were just beginning their spiritual journey and finding inclusion within the church.) There was also a sense in which this transition was ongoing, evolving and adapting in an ever changing world. I like McLaren's quote of Leadership Network's Netfax:

> *"Paradigm pliancy is the best strategy in times of rapid and turbulent change. Flexibility and a willingness to abandon outmoded methods and approaches are crucial. When the horse is dead, dismount."[53]*

There are many issues to be addressed when leading a congregation through transition. We have already dealt with three of them in previous chapters: environmental scanning, purpose and values. Other key issues we will discuss are: leadership, vision, strategy development, structures and evaluation. Throughout this discussion we will see the importance of the skills Wheatley suggests are important in the process of change: listening, conversing and

---

[52] Brian D McLaren, *The Church on the other Side*, Grand Rapids: Zondervan (2000), p19
[53] Brian D McLaren, *The Church on the other Side*, Grand Rapids: Zondervan (2000), p24

respecting people's uniqueness.[54]

Leadership

Effective leadership is essential to any organisation and in order for a congregation to be effective in transformation, the leadership will need to have a firm grasp of a transformational agenda. Roxburgh and Romanuk write of the need for missional leaders whose eyes are focussed on the kingdom and whose energies are devoted towards the empowerment of people. [55]

At BCLC the leadership endeavoured to turn the eyes of the church outwards to see the need for God's kingdom to come into the community and to help each member to find their purpose in that missional process. Empowerment leads to fulfilment.

As Roxburgh and Romanuk comment, "Missional leadership is about creating an environment within which the people of God in a particular location may thrive."[56]

The Reformation leaders failed to reform the Christendom models of structure and ministry which has been adopted by Protestant groups ever since, although different names are used. I used to be a fairly typical 'pastor' of a church, the one person ultimately responsible for

---

[54] Margaret Wheatley, *Leadership and the New Science*, San Francisco: Berret-Koehler (2006), pp39
[55] TIM notes, Module 406.1 *Mission History*, p2
[56] Roxburgh & Romanuk, *The Missional Leader*, San Francisco: Jossey-Bass (2006), p6

everything. The elders and deacons helped to support my numerous and diverse activities, but my main emphases were maintenance and management because there was little time for anything else. "Management without visionary leadership leads to ministry that is mechanical, passionless, predictable and limited".[57]

Many churches see the pastor as the anointed person who controls everything and makes all the decisions. William Easum distinguishes between oppressive control structures, which he believes are on their way out, and freeing permission-giving structures that are emerging. He recognises these latter structures as empowering, enabling people to explore their spiritual gifts on behalf of the body of Christ. [58]

Leadership in the New Testament is usually in the context of plurality. The singular word 'Pastor' does not actually occur in the New Testament. The only time we find that term is in Ephesians 4 when Paul is talking about the various ministries God has given to the church, 'some to be pastors'.[59] All the way through the Acts of the Apostles we find the practice of setting up elders in churches as the leadership[60]. In Jerusalem they had the apostles and elders[61]. Paul

---

[57] Barna George, *Turnaround Churches*, California: Regal Books (1993), p35
[58] Quoted in McLaren Brian, *The Church on the Other Side*, Grand Rapids: Zondervan (2000), p105
[59] Ephesians 4:11, NKJV
[60] Acts 14:23; 20:17; 1Tim 5:17, James 5:14, NKJV
[61] Acts 15:2,4,6,22, NKJV

talks in his letters about establishing elders in churches[62]. In today's terminology that would be a team. Therefore it could be argued that a core team or eldership each contributing from their individual gift mix into the leading of the church is the more Biblical approach to senior leadership.

This can be very threatening to a pastor. Particularly one that has been a pastor in the traditional sense I have referred to. Such pastors can be the biggest block to effective mission because of their desire for control. If pastors control things, the consequential danger is limited empowerment for other members of the congregation, limited building of a strong leadership team, limited delegation and limited use of the gifts people have. Roxburgh and Romanuk wisely comment on the need to move away from the CEO style of leadership that has everything worked out and instead cultivate an environment where the 'missional imagination' of God's people can be released. [63]

As BCLC began to change the way it did things and release people into their God ordained functions – I both rejoiced and went through an identity crisis at the same time. I realised that my identity was in what I did, rather than who I was. False equations I was subconsciously living by surfaced:

Performance + Accomplishments = Significance

[62] Titus 1:5, NKJV
[63] Roxburgh & Romanuk, *The Missional Leader*, San Francisco: Jossey-Bass (2006), p21

Status + Recognition = Security

Appearance + Admiration = Acceptance[64]

I like the way Alan Roxburgh puts it:

> *"In transition a whole world comes unglued. Individuals or communities feel disconnected and uprooted from ways of life they love, loyalties that gave meaning to their lives and habits that made sense. These changes keep us off balance, underscoring the experience of being out of control. Assumed values, once took for granted, are called into question as they no longer seem to work in the in-between world. Accepted moorings become broken havens."[65]*

For example, when someone else was hired to focus on community, I felt they were taking a little bit of me away.

I now understand that I was going through the process of 'liminality' as I was separated from my known world and finding myself outside many of my familiar frameworks. The identity and roles that gave life meaning and purpose were no longer there. There was a resulting confusion, bewilderment, depression and a feeling that my identity had been stolen. I was no longer sure who I was or what I was

---

[64] Steve Goss, *Freedom in Christ Discipleship Course*, Reading: FICM UK (2006), Session 1
[65] TIM notes, Module 406.3 *The Management and Culture of Change*, p30

supposed to be doing.[66]

Allowing people who were better at certain activities than me to get on with their responsibilities and initiatives worked. People were released to be what God had shaped them to be including myself. Tom Marshall, in his book, 'Understanding Leadership', comments that the mistake often made in the Christian church 'is to equate leadership with ministry'[67], a crucial distinction.

The principles discussed here can be seen in Martin Robinson & Dwight Smith's book: 'Invading Secular Space'[68]. They argue that logically speaking – if there is one person at the top of a pyramidal leadership structure – the church (or any organisation) will die the death of the strengths and weaknesses of that person. Authoritarian leadership which controls everything, fails to team build and delegate, is not only ineffective but is not in line with New Testament leadership. Also, in our post-modern context, people respond better to relational authority than positional authority.

Robert Greenleaf, writing about how administration should be structured in a church in his book, Servant Leadership, comes to a similar conclusion about the liabilities of the 'single chief' structure and believes in authority being placed in a balanced team of equals

---

[66] TIM course notes, Module 406.3 *The Management and Culture of Change*, p36
[67] Tom Marshall, *Understanding Leadership*, Tonbridge: Sovereign World (1991), p6
[68] Robinson & Smith, *Invading Secular Space*, London: Monarch Books (2003), Chapter 7

under the leadership of a servant who serves as first amongst equals. [69]

The Purpose of New Testament Leadership

The ministry gifts of Ephesians 4:11-12 are clearly stated to be for equipping the church to do good works; for mobilising the army. Whilst we must be careful not to confuse leadership with ministry in this passage, I think it would be fair to say that the gifts referred to are those ideally present in a leadership team and so we can conclude that a primary purpose of New Testament leadership is empowerment. Therefore empowerment must, as we have been seeing, inform our understanding of missional leadership structures. The church needs all the gifts, either as a single congregation or part of a network. Congregations have tended to rely on the minister to supply nearly all the ministry and if the congregation is charismatic or Pentecostal, have looked for members of the congregation to use gifts they may have in the context of a Sunday service. It will depend on the primary gifting of the pastor as to what kind of church is grown.

This model of leadership has been around for so long, it seems normal. It is not normal. It is causing the church to stagnate and not fulfil its God given mandate effectively. It does not empower to produce a corporate impact on community.

---

[69] Robert K Greenleaf., *Servant Leadership*, New Jersey: Paulist Press (2002), p253

Frost and Hirsch go a stage further in seeing the fivefold ministry gifts of Ephesians 4:11 not only operating in the leadership of a local congregation but the congregation as a whole embracing them within its corporate life. They believe this is: "the antidote to the … hierarchical model that empowers certain leaders and disempowers the majority of Christians"[70].

Whilst this might be seen as a potentially revolutionary view, I would like to take this a stage further and suggest that these and other grace-gifts should also be embraced outside the corporate life of the church. They would then become truly missional in their operation and people would be extraordinarily empowered. I do not believe that the grace-gifts are to be hung-up on a peg when people leave the church building and only to be used on the premises. Such gifts are part of a Christian's make-up twenty-four hours a day!

The New Testament is full of empowering practices. The grace-gifts themselves are an example of God's commitment to empowerment and to mission. The model of discipleship and sending that Jesus used is a clear example. His was practice-based discipleship resulting in mission. I like this quote from Together in Mission course notes that demonstrates the premise that empowerment informs our understanding of missional structures:

---

[70] Michael Frost & Alan Hirsch, *The shaping of things to come: Innovation and Mission for the 21st Century Church,* (Massachusetts: Hendrickson, 2003), p225.

"Paul followed a similar pattern [to Jesus] of mission that was not based on ecclesiastical structures but on kingdom principles. For him, mission preceded church structures, which took their shape from the outcome of missional activity and the needs of converts. Paul didn't set out to win converts as much as to make disciples whose calling was to live out kingdom values. Their witness in alien cultures then produced fresh communities of faith."[71]

Another important task for transformational leaders is to begin the process of dismantling institutionalism. When I really began to question the things the church had been doing for a long time and asked, "why do we do them, is there a Biblical mandate for this?" I found some surprises. When Hezekiah became king, one of the first things he did was remove the bronze serpent that Moses had made. This artifact had served its purpose in the wilderness but had now become an item of worship. There are equivalent items of worship in our churches which take many forms, but are now obsolete and need breaking up.

Leaders need to expect to lose people in the process of change but expect to gain people when they begin to work towards the new vision. This is the most painful part of transitioning a congregation to become missional. People leave most of the time because of religious

---

[71] TIM notes, Module 406.4 *Mission and Empowerment*, p8

attitudes or because they perceive their personal needs are not being met. Some find change too difficult. There is a distinction between the changes themselves and the effects of those changes on the people concerned. Several people at BCLC initially embraced the changes that were set before them, but were unable to survive the effects those changes had on them.

Vision

A well known Biblical verse reminds us that without vision the people perish.[72] Henry Kissinger said, "If you do not know where you are going, every road will get you nowhere"[73]. Kotter says that, 'vision refers to a picture of the future with some implicit or explicit commentary on why people should strive to create that future'.[74] The picture of the future for a congregation needs to reflect its perceived nature and purpose. If this is mission (i.e. integral mission) the vision will capture the heart of God for community and motivate the congregation to transform into a vehicle to bring it about.

Vision is powerful. It unites people in heart and purpose, it energises and informs actions, it fosters risk taking, it enhances leadership, promotes excellence, it provides purposeful direction and it streamlines the whole approach to the church's mission in the world.

---

[72] Proverbs 29:18, KJV
[73] The Teal Trust, www.teal.org.uk (Dec. 2009)
[74] John P. Kotter, *Leading Change*, Boston: HBS Press (1996), p68

Wheatley argues that vision should not be conceived as designing the future or creating a destination for the organisation. "We have believed that the clearer the image of the destination, the more force the future would exert on the present, pulling us to that desired state". She sees this as strong 'Newtonian' thinking. If vision is a field it would have far more formative influence.

> When *"creating vision, we are creating a power, not a place, an influence, not a destination... we need congruency in the air, visionary messages matched by visionary behaviours... vision must permeate through the entire organisation as a vital influence on the behaviour of all employees... We would become an organisation of integrity, where our words would be seen and not just heard."*[75]

Defining and developing vision is a key role of leadership. It can be seen in the great Biblical leaders such as Moses[76], Joshua[77], David[78] and Nehemiah[79]. Tom Marshall in his book, 'Understanding Leadership', refers to foresight as being at the heart of leadership and foresight requires vision.[80]

[75] Margaret Wheatley, *Leadership and the New Science*, San Francisco: Berret-Koehler (2006), pp 55,56
[76] Exodus 4:29-31, NKJV
[77] Joshua 1:10-15, NKJV
[78] 1 Chron. 28, NKJV
[79] Neh. 2:17-18, NKJV
[80] Tom Marshall, *Understanding Leadership*, Tonbridge: Sovereign World (1991), p11

Leaders need to position themselves to be able to receive vision. Being a serious student of the scriptures and devoted to prayer as a lifestyle will tune spiritual senses to understand God's heart and be more able to hear his voice.

What may begin as a moment's inspiration can mature into revelation through further study and listening prayer. The account of the gathered prophets and teachers at Antioch reveals that clear direction for advancing God's work in the earth can come through patiently and prayerfully waiting in God's presence.[81] These primary means of receiving vision will almost always align together and help safeguard us from error. There are also secondary means of receiving vision such as dreams, prophetic utterances and significant moments in our lives, but all of these will need to be weighed against the primary sources.

Receiving vision may happen as an event, but it will take process to bring it to maturity. For example, when God revealed to the leadership at BCLC a vision of community transformation, they were overwhelmed at first by its scope and boldness. They found many scriptures that spoke to them about how to move forward. The fifty eighth chapter of Isaiah became a meaningful passage to them as they came to understand that they needed to regain the ground of social involvement that the church had lost over generations. They knew God was calling the church to become a leading influence within their

---

[81] Acts 13, NKJV

community continuing what Jesus had begun in the earth. Saturated with fresh revelatory momentum they gave themselves to pursue this vision.

The core team involved a wider leadership team in formulating a vision statement and its associated bullet points that explained the vision in easily understood, practical terms. The vision was preached with great enthusiasm and energy. Some people readily embraced what was being communicated, whilst others needed more time to absorb all that it might mean for them. Yet others found that this was not what they felt called to and needed to join themselves to other churches with which they had a greater empathy. Some find change too difficult.

Wheatley's field concept of vision helps us realise the importance of everybody embracing the vision, because incongruous acts have disintegrating effects on what we dream to accomplish.

> *"Vision statements move off the walls and into the corridors, seeking out every employee, every recess in the organisation... We need all of us out there stating, clarifying, reflecting, modelling, filling all of space with the messages we care about. If we do that, a powerful field develops..."*[82]

---

[82] Margaret Wheatley, *Leadership and the New Science*, San Francisco: Berret-Koehler (2006), p57

The momentum created by God-given vision in the human heart is forceful!

BCLC understood that this vision was a long term goal. It recognised that it would take strategy, organisation and planning to achieve. The congregations hearts were captured by the mission but people needed to engage their minds to adopt a structured approach; this could not all be accomplished immediately.

This is not to ignore the frequent and unplanned changes that occur in our world. The specific strategy may be less clear. Wheatley quotes Jack Welch, the legendary CEO of General Electric, as saying that in this world of constant flux, "predicting is less important than reacting".[83] BCLC found this to be important when applying for funding from secular sources. As Governments can be reactive in their policies and investments, aligning community transformation projects to current Government concerns is more likely to attract funding. For example, the church secured a £300,000 grant to build a family fitness centre, as fitness and fighting obesity was high on the government's agenda at the time.

Vision sustains people through difficult times. Every church walks through a measure of tragedy, sadness and disappointment, and the larger the church the more likely this will be true. When these times

---

[83] Margaret Wheatley, *Leadership and the New Science*, San Francisco: Berret-Koehler (2006), p38

come, having a compass that anchors us to fixed points helps us survive the storm.

Vision provides clear direction for the church and effective leaders are constantly helping people to find their place within the vision most suited to their gifts and abilities. This may sound like recruiting rather than releasing, however, when people truly find their fit according to the way God has shaped them, it is most fulfilling and empowering. This is an ideal that is not always possible, particularly in a small church with more limited opportunities over a larger one with multiple ministry teams. However, even in a small church, when the perspective of ministry is inclusive of the community around it, empowerment opportunities are far more readily available.

Once received, vision needs to be nurtured and developed if it is to become reality. Vision grows as it is embraced. This can be done through studying relevant scriptures, attending relevant conferences, making appropriate lifestyle choices, dialoguing with other envisioned people, visiting model churches and engaging in the very activities that are part of the vision.

Maintaining vision is also important. Leadership needs to protect the vision from unhelpful influences such as negative attitudes and sidetracking.

Pursuing and accomplishing vision comes at a price: sacrifice and commitment are part of the process. Such vision is important in inspiring the kind of action necessary for community transformation and consequently church growth.

BCLC's picture of the future was of a healthy, low crime, prosperous community where its people live without life-controlling problems in happy families and where salvation is common place. It contained Kotter's six characteristics of an effective vision, namely, imaginable, desirable, feasible, focused, flexible and communicable.[84]

This vision was beneficial to the 'customers, employees and investors' (the three groups Kotter refers to), in a congregational context.

The congregation's 'customers' were the people in the community who they served through integral mission. When the congregation was focused on their interests because its vision was deeply rooted in the reality of its 'product', it found more 'buyers' coming in.

The congregation's employees and volunteers were more fruitful and thus fulfilled because they could more easily be empowered through serving in ways that reflected their gifts, abilities, passion, experience and personality, given the wide range of activities available to them. Transformational vision draws more people into service. For example,

---

[84] John P. Kotter, *Leading Change*, Boston: HBS Press (1996), p72

Debbie[85] had lost all confidence and did not know what to do with her life. Debbie had looked after her invalid mother for many years and now that season was over. Debbie's daughter was a member of BCLC and suggested her mother get involved in volunteering there. Debbie began to help with reception duties. As confidence grew, it became clear that Debbie had much more to offer and began running computer and family history classes in the centre before taking on the responsibility of overseeing the adult education provision.

The congregations 'investors' will also be more inspired to contribute towards the capital and revenue costs. 'Investors' will not only include congregational members but possibly secular organisations and funders, such as local and national government who also share a common interest in community. In BCLC's own case, they received over £600,000 of grants from the Welsh Assembly and local government for revenue and capital funding for community projects.

The three missional values outlined by Martin Robinson[86] will be furthered through transformational vision and can be seen reflected in the above discussion.

Firstly, 'whatever God is going to do in the world, he is going to do through all of Christ's people, the church'. God never intended 20% of his people to serve the other 80% of his people who do nothing.

---

[85] The real name has been changed to provide anonymity
[86]TIM course notes, Module 406.1 *The Nature and Purpose of Church*, pp4-5

Perhaps those figures would work if the 80% are out in the community serving.

Secondly, 'whatever God is going to do in the world through all of Christ's people in the world, he is going to do through leaders who empower people as their first priority; leaders who see this as more important than their own giftedness'. This is a great challenge. As BCLC transitioned into empowerment and delegation, I no longer knew what was happening all the time – and others were doing what I was doing – and some of those things were things that I enjoyed doing. But if my enjoyment and security becomes more important than empowering other people then I am breaking an important missional value. Leadership's primary role is mobilization of the people and vision is where this begins.

Thirdly, 'whatever God is going to do in the world through all of Christ's people he is going to do through a decentralized structure'. In other words, it is not about just maintaining the church, it is about the church going out and being church in community.

Paul tells us in Ephesians that we are all God's workmanship created to do good works that he ordained. Those good works are more often than not out in community. Diverse community projects allow more people to use their gifts and abilities. People are already decentralized 99% of the time at home, at work and in the market-place. Vision and the relevant strategy, will help them lead purpose driven lives.

Strategy development

The vision informed BCLC's strategy and it began to make the necessary changes to move the congregation forward in its journey. Hundreds of thousands of pounds flowed into this vision of community transformation, enabling BCLC to build a modern, relevant community life centre in the place of the old church meeting hall, thus creating an extraordinary environment in which to work out the vision goals. Wheatley records Karl Weick's comments, "It is only when we act to implement something that we create the environment."[87]

Strategy development involves the question, 'How are we going to accomplish our vision?' Asking this question will facilitate greater understanding of the vision and values, provide a sense of momentum, enable proper investment of God's resources, enable pro-activity rather than reactivity, identify weaknesses, strengths and threats, face the reality of change with a healthy process, reveal trends and their implications and get the whole church on the same page.[88]

Early in the process of formulating the vision, BCLC established what it called a Strategic Planning Team. It realized that there were people in the congregation with various skills who were not necessarily in the leadership team that could be brought together to plan projects and

---

[87] Margaret Wheatley, *Leadership and the New Science*, San Francisco: Berret-Koehler (2006), p37,38
[88] Aubrey Malphurs, *Advanced Strategic Planning Method*, www.malphursgroup.com (Dec 2008)

take responsibility for various aspects to help bring the plan to completion. This group, which consisted of fifteen people remained in existence after the new building was completed and met from time to time when needed. For example, they met to plan the building of a Family Fitness centre that was an extension of the new centre. Their skills include town planning, medicine, architecture, interior design, engineering, project management, business management, building and sport management.

One of the most important considerations for strategic development for congregations engaging in a missional vision is to consider the structures of the church.

Structures

Empowerment Structures

What new structures are relevant for the church to reach today's postmodern society? Kiryjon Caldwell's statement as quoted by Brian McLaren is insightful: "Organisational structure is like a pair of shoes. You fit the shoes to the feet; you don't make the feet fit the shoes".[89] This analogy is meaningful when thinking of empowerment, which embraces the mobilisation of people, helping them onto their feet with appropriate shoes (structures) to walk their God given path.

---

[89] McLaren Brian, *The Church on the Other Side*, Grand Rapids: Zondervan (2000), p101

Defining Empowerment

A Catholic priest, Paulo Freire, first used the term 'empowerment' in the 1960's whilst working with peasants in Brazil. He discovered that even illiterate labourers quickly learned to read when they could see that it had direct relevancy to their lives. Reading gave them a powerful tool for changing their lives and the world around them as it unlocked their understanding. They had been empowered to become agents of change.

Management theorists such as Bennis, Nanus, and Kanter [90] took up empowerment as an organisational efficiency tool from the late 1980's due to the length of time it was taking to pass decisions up and down the hierarchical structures in a rapidly changing environment. Market forces could change during this lengthy process and the decision may no longer be relevant. This can be seen clearly in the computer industry in the late 1980's where large significant manufacturers who failed to respond to the quickly changing technological advances and trends are no longer in business, such as ICL and Digital.

The concept of empowerment led to the flattening of the pyramidal decision making structures allowing delegation of authority to employees at lower levels, thus reducing the time between diagnosing

---

[90] Jay A. Conger and Rabindra N. Kanungo, *The Empowerment Process: Integrating Theory and Practice,* Briarcliff Manor, NY: The Academy of Management Review, Vol. 13, No. 3 (Jul. 1988), p471

market opportunities and the implementation of solutions. In order for this to be successful, empowered employees needed to have a clear grasp of the corporate vision and agree to broad goals.[91]

These principles of empowerment and the consequential informing of structures can be seen in churches that are adapting to the changing environment around them. "...the church is ... called to relate the gospel to each cultural context in which it seeks to bear witness".[92]

The concept of empowering people to maximise their effectiveness in the body of Christ is an important New Testament principle. 'Man-at-the-top' thinking pervaded society through the Jewish religious system at the time of Jesus and the Roman political system. This culture is still all around us and also in the church. It is a culture which is unredeemable. It is not the culture intended for churches. The church's leadership model needs to be the opposite: servant leadership – relational and influential; empowering others; giving authority with responsibility away; forcing the pyramidal structure to become flatter.

Defining Structure

In the context of this book, I will confine the definition of structure in terms of BCLC's congregational setting. As will be seen later, BCLC

---

[91] TIM notes, Module 406.4 *Mission and Empowerment*, pp4-5
[92] Eddie Gibbs & Ian Coffey, *Church Next: Quantum Changes in Christian Ministry*, Nottingham: IVP, (2000), p36

developed the capacity within its structure to empower not only members of the congregation but also members of the public.

Herrington, Bonnen and Furr have developed a diagram of a congregational system consisting of a series of layers or concentric circles. In the middle of this system are 'mental models'. In the terminology of BCLC's congregation, they would relate to its 'DNA', that is, the purpose and values that provide momentum and direction. These inform the next level, the 'structure'. Herrington comments, "Structure, as defined here, is not limited to the church's organizational hierarchy, but also includes predictable ways of thinking and behaving."[93] The structure informs the 'trends' of the congregation, the current direction which would be the missional context of our discussions. In turn these trends will inform the actual 'events' or current activities.

Thus missional structure will include how leadership and decision making is accomplished, how people are organised to fulfil their functions and how people are trained, discipled and equipped in a missional congregation.

Brian McLaren's makes an important observation when writing about reinventing church in the ever changing world around us. He does not see the New Testament as a fixed, detailed blueprint to be applied to

---

[93] Herrington Jim, Bonem Mike & Furr James, *Leading Congregational Change; A practical Guide for the Transformational Journey*, Dallas: Jossy-Bass (2000), p146

all churches in all cultures at all times, but rather as a case study of how the early church adapted to the rapid change and new challenges it faced. The key word, he says, is adaptability. [94]

Instead of assuming the structures of the past we must be free to allow them to adapt to the missional demands of today. If empowerment is to inform our understanding of structures and in turn change them, the structures need to be flexible enough to respond. McLaren uses a simple but helpful analogy. He says that in the same way that our wardrobes are full of outgrown clothes, so our church files should be full of outgrown structural diagrams. These structures fulfilled their purpose for their time and we do not need to feel bad that they no longer fit.[95]

Leadership Structure

Paul makes it clear in 1 Cor. 12:7-27 that as the body of Christ, we are all in this together. Everyone has gifts for the common good of all, which are decided by the Holy Spirit to further God's purpose and no gift is more important than another.

This should tell us that leadership of some kind is widely distributed amongst the body of Christ. That the core leadership has the task of creating a culture in which everyone can find their gift and use it, not

---

[94] Brian McLaren, *The Church on the Other Side*, Grand Rapids: Zondervan (2000), p23
[95] Brian McLaren, *The Church on the Other Side*, Grand Rapids: Zondervan (2000), p107

just within the church to enable it to function but also in terms of mobilisation of the body. Christ's body needs to be on the move transforming and redeeming the culture around it.

God is a team. God the Father, God the Son and God the Holy Spirit show us a model of cooperation and coordination. It takes all three to empower, engage and mobilise the church into purpose. No part of the trinity is more senior than another. This is a good model to follow.

One of the common components that Wagner identifies in the 'new apostolic churches' that are growing is a new authority structure, "We are seeing a transition from bureaucratic authority to personal authority, from legal structure to relational structure, from control to coordination, from rational leadership to charismatic leadership".[96]

In a missional structure, leadership is functional, not positional. Each member of the leadership team will have a specific functional role. Leadership teams will function best when the foundational gifts of Ephesians 4:11, apostles, prophets, evangelists, pastors and teachers, are present either within the team or accessible by the team. In fact, when these giftings permeate through the whole congregation the congregation itself will be an apostolic, God-directed, missional, caring and learning community.[97]

---

[96] Peter C Wagner., *The New Apostolic Churches*, California: Regal Books (1998), p15
[97] TIM notes, Module 406.5 *From Vision to Reality*, p11

The gift mix of the team members should certainly provide variety and include such abilities as vision casting, administration, planning, recruitment, finance, and worship. The team will benefit the congregation by helping to involve the majority of the church in ministry, provide solidarity and a growth mentality and produce a continuous improvement environment.

The roles of the core leaders are primarily to continually present and develop the vision and encourage and empower the team. Vision, clarity of purpose, well defined roles and responsibilities, delegated authority and flexibility are all of paramount importance in the leadership team. This may be considered to be a very functional view of leadership that might be reminiscent of a business, however, with a balanced gift mix present, there should be no conflict in achieving the blend of biblical purposes the church has been commissioned with. In fact the leadership team will be better equipped to lead their own teams. All teams will have a clear understanding that they are part of a whole organism and work accordingly rather than with their own agendas.

If amongst the leadership there is no apostolic gift, someone needs to be found who has that gift and can be trusted, to help build. Although there are other definitions, I see the apostle like a church consultant, someone who can advise and help build leadership and cast vision.

I believe this apostolic gift was vital for BCLC's transition. Rob was looking for a safe haven to recuperate after a difficult time in another church and joined BCLC. A working relationship with me was already in existence through Rob's leading of worship in our Prayer Tower gatherings. As Rob became better known in the congregation, it soon became clear that he had an ability to build and train leadership. Those with leadership potential were identified and Rob ran the first 'Equipped to Serve' leadership training course for twenty potential leaders. This coincided with initial discussion on the future of BCLC and its buildings. It was this budding leadership team that helped formulate the vision and later many of them became team leaders for the missional structure that developed.

Rob was also a businessman and brought to the table expertise in business plans and marketing. God had provided the right man at the right time. However, it was important that Rob's gifts were recognised and released by secure and mature leadership as already discussed.

It is interesting to note that Rob is now providing apostolic help to many churches across Wales.

The church structure involved establishing the teams in four major departments. These departments would be the responsibility of four core leaders (elders); each core leader was responsible for their own department. It was this structure that defined the major change in my role as pastor. I found myself in a different place in terms of organisational functions and roles. No longer was I responsible for everything, I was only responsible for my department. The core leaders met weekly to discuss issues that affected all departments and provided the leadership and management that ensured the church progressed towards its vision. This core group understood they were all equal to each other and would only reach decisions by consensus. Whilst I chaired and provided an agenda for these weekly meetings, I was no longer seen as the one with the ultimate authority. The leadership has become empowered in its plurality.

Team Structure

Congregational structures need to be designed to facilitate mission not maintenance, empowerment not passivity. When a congregation has missional vision and a missional leadership with an ethos to empower, it then needs to form a structure in which to operate missionally. Such a structure will reflect the strategy whereby the vision will be realised. "It is surprising how difficult it can be for churches to move from structures that essentially depend on inviting people to come rather than equipping people to go".[98]

Integral mission allows great diversity of involvement thus providing an abundance of opportunities. These opportunities need to be organised and shaped according to the strategy the congregation is

---

[98] TIM notes, Module 406.1 *Mission History*, p41

following. "Strategy provides both logic and a first level of detail to show how a vision can be accomplished".[99]

After conducting the market research BCLC gradually formed a strategy of providing services around three main areas: health and fitness, education and family. A team structure was then developed to accommodate these and church related areas. Every member of the congregation was asked to join a team reflecting their main interest. Gibbs and Coffey refer to churches with such a structure as networking churches.[100]

Discipleship Structure

The concept of discipleship within the structure is crucial.

> *"It is becoming more and more apparent that the essential life and character of a congregation must be given attention before the 'doing' issues are described. In other words, primacy must be given to who we are rather than to what we do. The feel and impact of what we do is given validity by the internal vitality of congregational life."*[101]

The concept of empowerment will inform our understanding of discipleship structures. People need to be grounded in relevant,

---

[99] John P. Kotter, *Leading Change*, Boston: HBS Press (1996), p75
[100] Eddie Gibbs & Ian Coffey, *Church Next*, Nottingham: IVP (2001), p90
[101] TIM notes, Module 406.1 *Mission History*, p46

practical Christianity, trained and equipped to serve. This will be done through a variety of ways including teaching, example and mentoring.

As part of BCLC's structure there was a training programme built in. This consisted of the Alpha Course where people are given the opportunity to explore the basics of Christianity; following this was the Freedom in Christ course, a discipleship course designed to firmly establish who people are in Christ and to rid themselves of past baggage that is inappropriate to the abundant life Jesus came to bring; this was then followed by a 'Shape' course that helped people discover how God had shaped them for the service (ministry) he had prepared for them. We also had a leadership training academy, where team and small group leaders were equipped to serve through leadership responsibility. "Discipleship is not complete until each individual has discovered their unique giftedness and is exercising that gift in a ministry of some kind." [102] This discovery process has to be part of discipleship, however, both the process and discipleship will never be complete as individuals continue the life-long quest to become more like Jesus.

The 'Shape' course referred to above was based on Rick Warren's material and provided teaching and tools to discover people's spiritual gifts, passion, abilities, personality and experiences which make them unique. Warren makes the point that people "will be most effective and fulfilled when they use their spiritual gifts and abilities in the area

---

[102] TIM notes, Module 406.1 *Mission History*, p38

of their heart's passion in a way that best expresses their personality and experiences". [103]

One of the problems with this packaged discipleship training programme was the length of time it took to complete. It took nearly a year if an individual attended all three courses consecutively.

BCLC also realised the importance of relationship within community as the congregation grew in numbers. They established small groups where people were able to interact socially and spiritually. The importance of building close relationships was highlighted by new people finding it difficult to be part of church community when they were unable to immediately see an area they could serve in or were not at an emotional place to do so. It is important to bridge the gap between purely organisational and organic structures.

The role of structure has been underestimated in its capacity to influence the success or effectiveness of church ministry.[104] McManus describes the work of leadership as 'design engineering' in relationship to developing structure, 'The ability to design efficient and economical structures, processes and systems is critical to maximising the power of momentum.'[105]

The missional vision needs to permeate through all teams, groups and

---

[103] Warren Rick, Class 301,see www.pastors.com
[104] TIM notes, Module 406.5 *From Vision to Reality*, p26
[105] Erwin McManus, *An Unstoppable Force*, Orange: Group Publishing (2001), p136

functions to keep the congregation on track. For example, homegroups, should they exist, need to be reminded of their missional existence even if they have pastoral, teaching, worship or other functions. The overall structure and its parts need always to be mindful of its reason for existence and be looking outwards, not inwards.

Once the church has developed and is implementing its strategy through the appropriate structures, it is time to plan for any contingencies that could neutralize or destroy the strategy.[106] For example, endeavouring to hold three months operational costs in the bank for contingency purposes, or making painful decisions to make people redundant to avoid slipping into financial difficulties. Leadership also need to start asking the 'What if' questions and discussing answers. For example, what if a group hostile to Christianity wants to hire your premises? The answers to such questions may take some time to think through. A thorough theological reflection of such questions was a core issue in BCLC's approach. The fundamental principles covered in chapter one need to be applied when thinking through such topics.

Evaluation

Some of the important roles of leaders involve reviewing, evaluating

---

[106] Aubrey Malphurs, *Planting growing churches*, Grand Rapids: Baker Books, (1998), p188

and redesigning in order to drive operational improvement while pursuing a clear strategy; to measure progress against the strategy and value delivered; and to maintain discipline around the strategy, in the face of many distractions.[107]

Structures need to be adaptable to the changing environment they are designed to serve. Hammer talks about two systems every organisation needs: surface and deep.

> *"The surface system focuses on the organised tasks of the business processes, with their attendant structures, systems, and values. But this system is periodically in need of major change, this is the job of the deep system... it monitors, governs, adjusts and reforms the surface system that creates customer value. The deep system bears the responsibility for detecting external changes, determining what those mean and intervening to modify the surface system..."[108]*

In BCLC's structure the deep system would have equated to the core leadership and the surrounding team structure, the surface system. The core leadership monitors, adjusts and reforms the surrounding structures, systems and values not just when major change is necessary, but when minor changes are required. It is important that structures have the capacity to support fresh initiatives and therefore

---

[107] Michael Porter, *The Global leadership Summit* 2007, Willow Creek.
[108] Michael Hammer, *Beyond Reengineering*, New York: Harper Collins, (1996), p9

it is vital that individuals who make up those structures are taught to adapt to change quickly.

Like the shoe analogy we used earlier, when the feet have grown, new shoes will be needed. If the structure no longer adequately supports empowering people for mission it needs to change.

Leadership need to be always asking the question, 'Are the structures in place serving the vision and enabling effective progress?' If not they need to be changed.

Constant review and revisiting the DNA of the vision will help to maintain it within the hearts of the those who make up the congregation. The demands of life at home, at church and at work can cause vision to drift without regular review.

Leaders can always be learning, redesigning and transitioning. From the acquisition of knowledge and information from both inside and outside the church, they can create, design and install new ways of working [109] and can set specific goals each year that are designed to further the vision and can be evaluated at the end of the year. Team leaders can complete an annual appraisal which is a useful tool in keeping the leaders and their teams in pursuit of the corporate vision and provides an opportunity to evaluate each department's effectiveness.

---

[109] Michael Hammer, *Beyond Reengineering*, New York: Harper Collins, (1996), p9

Documentation of steps and processes of transition.

Change can be described as the move from one state to another and the action steps that take place. Transition is the psychological stage and process which enables people to make the change.[110]

The steps and processes BCLC went through to achieve its change and transition were accelerated to a large extent by its building programme. The need to replace the main worship area which had passed its use-by date kick started a process. The stimulus for initial change was a crisis. The principles of leading change would have been more difficult to adopt and implement without a major project to focus on. On the other hand, a slower pace of transition may have resulted in less people being lost from the congregation. Fifty percent of the congregation eventually left to join various other churches in which they felt more comfortable, but within a couple of years the congregation tripled in size (at least twice the size of the original congregation). The 'innovators', 'early adopters' and 'early majority' groups did not have time to influence some of the 'late majority' and 'laggards'.[111] Some in the latter groups were unable to accept the cultural changes being made to the congregation. "Stalwarts in a dying church often argue that things will return to normal if the church can do a better job of doing what it has always done"[112] and resist the

---

[110] TIM notes, Module 406.3 *The Management and Culture of Change*, p29
[111] TIM notes, Module 406.3 *The Management and Culture of Change*, p24
[112] George Barna, *Turnaround Churches*, Ventura: Regal Books (1993), p37

changes that are necessary.

Kotter's eight stage process of change

Kotter describes in detail an eight stage process of creating major change. Before elaborating on this process, he says that:

> *"needed change can still stall because of inwardly focused cultures, paralyzing bureaucracy, parochial politics, a low level of trust, lack of teamwork, arrogant attitudes, lack of leadership in middle management, and the general fear of the unknown'".*[113]

To some extent all these obstacles were present before BCLC began its transition, but were gradually dealt with during the process of change.

Kotter's first stage is establishing a sense of urgency.

In the congregational life cycle outlined by Alice Mann, a stability phase will be followed by a decline and eventually death if nothing is done about it. This decline can be stopped and a rise towards stability can be achieved through revisiting the formative questions again: Who are we? What has God called us to do or be? Who is our neighbour?[114]

Before its transition, BCLC had enjoyed a period of stability, but was in

---

[113] John P. Kotter, *Leading Change*, Boston: HBS Press (1996), p20
[114] Alice Mann, *Can our church live?: Redeveloping congregations in decline*, Bethesda, Md.: Alban Institute (1999), Chapter 1

grave danger of decline because of a lack of conversions. The community had become 'word resistant' and showed little interest in the gospel. The building was in need of major repair or rebuild.

These factors helped build a sense of urgency, something needed to be done and Mann's formative questions began to be asked. BCLC needed to overcome a degree of complacency, holding on to the status quo of low performance standards and thinking everything was satisfactory.

One missional change principle is learning how to discern what God is doing in, through and among all the movements in which congregations find themselves.[115] This will involve looking at the wider world and what God is doing globally. One of the defining moments for me and subsequently for the congregation was seeing the Transformation videos produced by George Ottis Jr and the Senitel Group showing communities and nations undergoing dramatic transformation. I also had the 'Eureka' moment during one of our monthly all night prayer meetings that I have already referred to, when I realised that God wanted us to play our part in transformation, not just pray about it. Philip Greenslade believes that the starting point for all great movements of God in history has been revelation. Leaders need to know who God is and where he wants to take his people.[116]

The next real step towards change at BCLC began when a group of

---

[115] TIM notes, Module 406.3 *The Management and Culture of Change*, p34

[116] Philip Greenslade, *Leadership*, Basingstoke: Marshalls Paperbacks (1984), p41

about twenty potential leaders were identified and trained as previously described. In Kotter's terminology this equated to his second stage, 'creating the guiding coalition'. The numbers being trained were far more than were needed at the time, but the necessity to build for the future rather than just for the present was realised. A bigger future would require a bigger leadership. An in-house leadership training course was used. Part of the course involved creating, planning, organising and running a Christmas event with a budget and using some of the principles taught on the course. This was a powerful team building tool and resulted in an excellent, successful event and a degree of trust in the team.

The training resulted in a team that became the leaders of various teams that were later to develop. They were instrumental in driving the changes forward. Later, a core leadership of four materialised that was more akin to Kotter's concept of a guiding coalition. The core leadership had a strong position of power, broad expertise, and high credibility with leadership and management skills.[117] Meeting weekly, the core leadership team led and managed various projects within the main project.

Kotter's third stage is the development of vision and strategy. Part of the leadership training course entailed casting the vision. This involved clarifying the direction of change, where BCLC was going and

---

[117] John P. Kotter, *Leading Change*, Boston: HBS Press (1996), p66

motivating and coordinating action. I had a firm idea of what the vision for the church should be, but it was important for the leadership team to work out how to vocalise it, so that they could own it. A vision statement was produced followed by bullet points describing what it meant in practice. These statements were to be easily understood by un-churched people.

The vision statement was: 'to see the village of Cefn Cribwr and the surrounding region transformed for the glory of God'. The transformation would include seeing sick people healed, families reconciled and happy, people free of addictions, the end of abuse of all kinds, the crime rate reduced and the community prospering.

"The bridge between the past and the future is the strategic philosophy that filters ideas, plans and activities."[118]As BCLC cast its vision, it realised that God was changing its focus away from event orientated evangelism to process oriented service. The strategy for transformation would be serving the community out of love for the people. The congregation needed to work on building relationships and bridges into the community. It was believed that as it did this and engaged in integral or holistic mission, salvation would follow. BCLC had produced an ambitious, clear, imaginable and appealing picture of the future and logic for how the vision could be achieved.

The leadership were now able to begin communicating this vision to

---

[118] George Barna, *Turnaround Churches*, Ventura: Regal Books (1993), p74

the congregation. Kotter commences his chapter on his fourth stage, communicating the change vision, by saying that the real power of a vision is released only when most of those involved have a common understanding of the organisation's goals, direction and future.[119]

The leadership used multiple means of communicating the vision. It produced a large poster to be seen by all entering the building and smaller leaflets for all to have. It preached, prayed, taught and discussed the vision. It showed examples of what this vision could look like. It attended conferences where this type of vision was talked about. It placed the vision on a weekly news bulletin. It visited the sceptics to hopefully persuade them to run with the vision. It understood the paradigm shift the vision would demand and the need to keep repeating and communicating it in ways everybody could understand. Every meeting of the congregation will reflect the vision in some way. It was surprising how few congregants could really articulate the vision even after such repetitive communication. It is easy to underestimate the degree of psychological transition people may be going through.

Now BCLC had a clear vision and a leadership team to help implement it, the function of the new building that was being designed was much clearer. Instead of building another church for the congregation, a

---

[119] John P. Kotter, *Leading Change*, Boston: HBS Press (1996), p85

multi-purpose centre that would serve the community needed to be built.. This was a most important decision, because the mounting cost of the project was outside BCLC's ability to finance, but it was able to secure a handsome grant from the Welsh Assembly of £220,000 which represented about two thirds of the cost, because they were willing to fund a community project that would serve the area with needed resources.

As the building began to take shape and its various functions thought through, BCLC were able to move to Kotter's fifth stage, empowering employees (volunteers in this case) for broad-based action, by mobilising the congregation into teams and utilising members of the leadership team as team leaders. The empowerment process was also aided by the congregant's contribution to the new building costs which resulted in a sense of ownership and commitment. Buying in to the project in this way was important for the psychological transition people needed to make.

Kotter describes his sixth step as 'generating short term wins'. BCLC did not set out to deliberately do this, as Kotter suggests you should, but there were a number of wins during the process that helped build morale and motivation, justify the short-term costs, provide concrete data on the viability of the project, make it more difficult for people to argue against the change and turning neutrals into supporters and reluctant supporters into active helpers.[120] "Success breeds success; it breaks down people's reluctance to get involved and lures them back to involvement in ministry".[121]

BCLC's wins included receiving the Welsh Assembly grant; a sympathetic building contractor who held his price while the finance was sought; the right people being available at the right time to staff the project; and the subsequent growth in numbers using the centre and coming to the church. The £300,000 grant for the construction of the Family Fitness centre and numerous smaller grants from time to time. BCLC was used by the Welsh Government as a model for community regeneration, it received the Queen's Award for voluntary service (equivalent to an MBE for an organisation), an award for 'green' practices in the work place and was appointed economic champions in recognition of the sustainable nature of our project. It also regularly saw people's lives transformed.

For example, the local comprehensive school contacted BCLC and asked if it would consider helping a pupil who was on the verge of exclusion for serious anger management issues. Jack[122] came to the centre four days a week and over a period of two years, staff members worked with Jack and his anger management issues as he worked in various areas of the centre. He responded well in the empowering

---

[120] John P. Kotter, *Leading Change*, Boston: HBS Press (1996), p123
[121] George Barna, *Turnaround Churches*, Ventura:Regal Books (1993), p80
[122] The real name has been changed to provide anonymity

environment and the school were amazed at his progress. Jack later attended the local technical college and achieved good qualifications. He was very grateful for BCLC's investment into his life.

It would be amiss of me not to mention at this point, that these 'wins' were not so much BCLC's, but God's. "Faith stories are God at work moments".[123]

Throughout the process outlined above, relevant Biblical teaching on the changes introducing took place. (See Appendix 1). Much was made of the 'crossing over' experiences of the Israelites under the leadership of Joshua, as they entered the Promised Land. Everything was different on the other side of the Jordan. As Joshua told the people, "you have not passed this way before."[124] This teaching helped the congregation to begin to prepare for the major changes that were about to happen, but for many, religious attitudes and a life-time of church being primarily for them rather than for others prevented them from 'crossing over' with us and they joined other churches that they felt more comfortable in.

Those who stayed were able to experiment and implement the fourth stage of Everett Rogers' model, that is, they learnt to put the innovation to use and thus initiate new practices in the congregation.

---

[123] Dan Southerland, *Transitioning*, Grand Rapids: Zondervan (2002, p92
[124] Joshua 3:4, NKJV

BCLC remained in Rogers' final stage, 'confirmation-reinforcement', for some time. The people continued to practice the implementation of the new innovation, they grew in their ability to function with new practices; they came to recognize that they were operating in a new way. The continued positive outcomes embedded themselves as new habits in the congregation. [125]

Closely aligned to Rogers' fourth stage is Kotter's seventh, 'consolidating gains and producing more change'. Encouraged by what had been achieved, BCLC completed another major building project with its sights set on yet another in the future. Additional people were brought in, promoted, and developed to help with all the changes; this included both paid and volunteer staff. The core leadership continued to maintain clarity of shared purpose for the whole project and kept urgency levels up. They gave more responsibility to some personnel. The team structure described above helped to remove some unnecessary interdependencies.[126]

Kotter's final stage involves 'anchoring new approaches in the culture'. During BCLC's transition reference was made to the new culture as the 'DNA' of the church. It is what makes it tick. This DNA reflected values and takes time to filter through everything that is done, said and down to the core identity. Church growth presents the need to be continually

---

[125] TIM notes, Module 406.3 *The Management and Culture of Change*, p27
[126] John P. Kotter, *Leading Change*, Boston: HBS Press (1996), p143

presenting this DNA to new people as well as reminding those who have been around a while.

Putting the principles into practice

As seen earlier from my own inner responses to transition the experience of liminality can be bewildering. The resulting 'threshold experience' of tension between wanting to recover the lost past but discover an alternative future can result in confusion, anger, discomfort, an instinctive desire to re-capture the old world and a sense that our lives are out of control and threatened.[127] Helping people through this emotional transitional state was something BCLC did not pay enough attention too. It treated the transition like the change and made the mistake of just feeding people with information and getting them to commit to playing their role in the new. If it had understood liminality at the time, it may have avoided losing so many people in the transition process. However, the clear vision and strategy got plans off the ground and shaped the future.

Throughout this transitional process the leadership encouraged the congregation to see the community not as a potential place for church growth but as a place where it is called to enter with listening love.[128]

While the roadmap to the full planning process appears linear, like any

---

[127] TIM notes, Module 406.3 *The Management and Culture of Change*, p37
[128] TIM notes, Module 406.3 *The Management and Culture of Change*, p36

good conversation, it will have its own natural flow.

It helps to think of the planning process as having three phases. In the book Holy Conversations each of these phases is described in detail. They are firstly getting ready by preparing the people to plan, secondly gathering relevant information and finally shaping the future.[129]

In this chapter we have described in much detail the process of transitioning the church from its rather inward looking, hierarchical and traditional ways to a more outward, kingdom orientated, empowered congregation.

In the final chapter we will look at what BCLC became during the ten year period between the start of transition and when I left. The process of change always continues and is therefore never complete. Ten years is a comparatively short period to make qualitative assessments as to the effectiveness of the transition on the community, however, there were signs of change which I will present.

---

[129]The Alban Institute, www.holyconversations.org (Dec. 2009)

Chapter 5 After transition

Service provision

In Chapter 1, I detailed the typical week and service provision of BCLC before its transition. There follows an outline of the service provision after transition. I have included a more detailed description for interest in Appendix 5.

Service	Provision
Oasis Coffee Bar	Mon – Fri 10am – 3pm
Family Fitness Centre	70 hours a week
Large Main Hall	Multipurpose 7 days a week
Excel Sports (Sport for the disabled)	3 sessions per week
2 Tennis Courts	Available by arrangement
Parent and Toddlers	Two sessions weekly
Children's clubs	2 sessions weekly + Summer clubs
Young people's clubs	3 sessions weekly + Summer club
Youth outreach (Street work)	2 sessions weekly
Sunday clubs for children	4 groups on Sunday mornings

Counselling (by qualified counsellors)	Mon – Thu by appointment
Community Connections Project	Collection and delivery of household furniture using rented warehouse. Practical help for homeless, drug addicts, poor and lonely.
Adult Education Courses	Wide variety of courses some OCN accredited Mon to Fri.
Dorcus Group	Senior Citizens group providing gifts and clothing to mainly the poor in Eastern Europe. 1 session weekly
Modern Relevant Church	Various programmes and courses throughout week.
DigiLab	Digital equipment centre primarily used by young people
Mini Bus (with disabled access)	Used throughout the

	week
Conferencing, Meetings, Catering, weddings, parties	5 fully equipped rooms of various sizes (max:300) for hire
School work	Assemblies, after school clubs, health & fitness, coaching those not attending.
Overseas Projects	Sponsoring work and schools in Brazil, Uruguay and Poland.

Staff

Before transition, I was the only paid worker on staff. Now the payroll is as follows:

> Church Minister (full time)
>
> Community Focus Manager/Centre Manager (full time)
>
> Sports Coordinator/Youth Manager (full time)
>
> Children's Coordinator (part time)
>
> Three Gym Instructors (part time)
>
> Self Employed Church Consultant (part time)
>
> Two Youth Workers (Part-time)

In addition to paid staff, there are a number of full time and part time volunteers:

Building Use & Project Manager

Treasurer

Admin Manager

Booking Clerk

Two professional counsellors

More than 50 volunteers including Team Leaders of various functions

Sunday service

It is clear to see that the church radically changed in its involvement with the community. The congregation reached about one hundred and fifty people meeting on a Sunday morning. When the congregation met for the first time in the new building five years previous, the number was approximately fifty.

The Sunday morning service became very different to what it was. The aim was to provide an inclusive service that anyone could benefit from. The worship was contemporary with a band leading it. There were three screens and projectors and lighting to provide multi-media presentation. The preaching was practical, applying Biblical principles into everyday life. For example, I preached a series of talks about attitudes under the general strap-line, 'Great attitude, great life'. This gave me an opportunity to preach on our attitude to many topics, for example, authority, money, time, service, relationships. Whether people had been Christians for years or had not started their journey yet, everyone was able to take something away from the teaching to enhance their life.

Prayer was offered, particularly for physical healing, after the service.

People were often given the opportunity to ask Jesus to be their Lord and people regularly did so. For example, Kate[130] had been a member of BCLC for three years. A depressed single mum struggling to find purpose and meaning to life came to the Alpha course, which introduces Christianity to people. Kate's life changed for the better through the loving support of people at BCLC; she became a Christian, the depression lifted and a zest for life returned with a desire to make a difference in the world for others.

This chapter has briefly outlined BCLC's multiple service provision which evolved during its transition.

The quantifiable outcomes of transition grew as BCLC continued its journey towards community transformation. Transformation is normally a slow process, however, it was hoped a tipping point would be reached at some stage when the process would accelerate. In Appendix six I have documented some outcomes illustrated by some moving stories, but there were many more outcomes that were un-

---

[130] The real name has been changed to provide anonymity

measurable and lying underneath the surface of the community like seeds waiting to burst through into the light.

After transition, published crime figures for Cefn Cribwr showed a 50% reduction in crime. (See Appendix seven). Whilst BCLC cannot claim to be the reason for this reduction, I believe the work in the community, especially amongst young people had a bearing on this. A reduction in crime was one of the stated objectives in BCLC's vision statement.

Transformation of community will involve individual lives being transformed. Such as Steve[131] who, eighteen months previous, was a homeless alcoholic living in a ruined vicarage in a neighbouring village. He was aged forty two and had been an alcoholic for twenty years. He was estranged from his family and heavily in debt. He came into the centre one weekday and was given food, a shower and fresh clothes. BCLC continued to provide regular help for several weeks. Steve then had a serious accident and was hospitalized for three months. During this time I regularly visited him and took care of his administration. Over a year period, I invested much mentoring time and practical help into Steve and he became a transformed man: saved, almost debt free and dry. He became involved in volunteering in the centre most days, married at BCLC and attended a Christian rehabilitation unit that helped him re-programme his pressure coping

---

[131] The real name has been changed to provide anonymity

mechanisms.

The other transformed lives recorded in Appendix six and the many more not mentioned happened because of the principles discussed in this book being put into practice. Perhaps the overriding factor determining individual transformation was a willingness at BCLC to demonstrate unconditional love in a sacrificial way.

Conclusion

Roxburgh and Romanuk note how the destabilization of culture constitutes discontinuous change that leaves congregants feeling as though their world is spinning.

> *"We are in a global-risk society where traditional means of forming life (family, church, nation, business, law, and politics) have been drained away; leaving a world that appears without direction".*[132]

How crucial, therefore, that churches engage with the communities around them as they are one of the few places where there remains the possibility of re-engaging a larger narrative. In order for this to happen, change and transition must happen. Leading change is a complex and time consuming process, but without it, the paradigm shifts necessary for church survival will not occur.

---

[132] Roxburgh & Romanuk, *The Missional Leader*, San Fransisco: Jossey-Bass (2006), p67

Peter Wagner, in his book, 'The New Apostolic Churches' which is all about the changing face of Christianity, comments that:

"Every time Jesus began building his Church in a new way throughout history, he provided new wineskins...The growth of the Church through the ages is, in part, a story of new wineskins".[133]

Three major forms of change can all be seen in this case study. The change in identity as the church responded to its environment and forged new relationships. The change in organisation as the church developed new ministry priorities to meet the challenge of social changes in the environment. The change in structure and governance as the leadership created teams, became 'flatter', and delegated operational authority to the team leaders.[134] This provided multiple serving opportunities both inside and outside the church and a discipleship structure that supported, trained and equipped people to recognise and fulfil their God given shape.

Such empowerment through networking structures is appropriate in post-modernity. The relational permission-giving authority and mutual accountability these structures offer will attract more willing participants to them, than the authoritarian, controlling hierarchical ones of the past. Gibbs and Coffey comment:

---

[133] Peter C.Wagner, *The New Apostolic Churches*, Ventura: Regal Books (1998), p15
[134] TIM notes, Module 406.3 *The Management and Culture of Change*, p21

"Within a fragmented and variegated post-modern society the church will need to diversify its ministries and release its financial and human resources to develop ministries appropriate for each population segment".[135]

Successful transition lies in good leadership that seeks and develops God imparted missional vision and values which will drive congregations forward to become a transforming influence. It is important to continually sow a pioneering mentality into the 'DNA' of the church. There always needs to be a fresh, excellent and relevant edge to all that churches do in the future. Leadership need not be afraid of change and radical obedience to the word of God. Rather, change and obedience open up greater opportunity to influence society. Churches that are focused away from themselves are more likely to make the most of the time they have left on earth. They understand their missional purpose.

However, to fulfil purpose and enable vision to become reality requires defining and working hard through the processes described above. This is not for the faint hearted. It requires courageous, strong, faith-filled leadership teams that inspire congregations to become visionary, God-directed, missional communities that are continually learning and transitioning to become the salt and light of the world.

---

[135] Eddie Gibbs & Ian Coffey, *Church Next*, Nottingham: IVP (2001), p90

As BCLC embarked on a one way journey towards missional church, other congregations were inspired to follow. My hope is that eventually we will reach a 'tipping point' where multiplication will begin. Margaret Mead, a US anthropologist said, "Never doubt that a small group of thoughtful, concerned citizens can change the world. Indeed, it is the only thing that ever has." [136]

We certainly need a movement of missional congregations that have understood the need for a paradigm shift in their mode of operation. I am delighted BCLC embarked on its transitional journey; the service provision, outcomes and numerical growth of the church was satisfying.

The potential for world changing mission is within the grasp of the church. If every church member was empowered to play their part in integral mission activity, taking up serving towels and willingly serving other people in their everyday lives in diverse ways, such attitudes and actions could transform our communities.

In its community BCLC has been involved in housing the homeless, bringing freedom to addicts, feeding the hungry, clothing the poor, educating adults, mentoring young people, teaching children, counselling the dysfunctional, helping people become more healthy, providing relevant facilities and serving in many other ways. As Bill

---

[136] Margaret Mead (1901-1978) www.interculturalstudies.org (Dec 2009)

Hybels observed, "People who are far from God are rarely more impacted than when they see 21st century Christ-followers behaving as Christ behaved."[137]

In our 'Quantum Age' as Easum terms it, where change has become discontinuous and chaotic,[138] the structures will need to be constantly evaluated and flexibility built in for swift change. There will always need to be room in these structures for more people to be empowered. Indeed, the potential for growth is much greater as more people are empowered to take initiative.

Such is the importance of the principles in this book that it could be argued they hold keys to the survival of many churches in the West.

---

[137] Bill Hybels, *The Volunteer Revolution: Unleashing the Power of Everybody* Grand Rapids: Zondervan (2004), Back Cover.
[138] Eddie Gibbs & Ian Coffey, *Church Next*, Nottingham: IVP (2001), p89

Afterword

Should you visit BCLC today, you will not find it as described in Chapter 5. When I left in 2012 a new leadership team took over which did not share the vision and values or exercise the principles of structure and empowerment outlined in this book. A new leader steered a very different ship and sadly many of the church members of my day will now be found in other local churches.

The reasons for my resignation and how a new leadership came about is complex and beyond the scope of this book. A transformational vision can take sometime to form and be assimilated into a congregation, but it can be easily lost without consistency of leadership and in turn the long term process of community transformation can be stalled.

Appendix 1

Teaching transition from the Bible

Leaders need to teach and inspire missionally. Transitioning a church into a new 21st century relevant missional model needs to be taught. People need to understand the Biblical mandate.

We have already made many references to the Bible to establish a mandate for transitioning church for transforming community, particularly in chapter 3 of this book. To help leaders tasked with teaching transition I have included this Appendix to give further insight into material used.

Key texts for community engagement:

There is a rich source of text in scripture to substantiate community engagement. There are some eight hundred passages dealing with the issues of justice and righteousness alone. God is clearly concerned for the oppressed and needy in society and looks for the church to be too. In this section I will briefly highlight what I consider to be some key texts.

Fundamental to our existence and role on this planet is our ruling of it.[139] Planet housekeeping is mankind's responsibility and therefore there is a clear green agenda for Christians to play their part in this. God designed a beautiful sustainable world for everybody and the

---

[139] Gen 1:26-27 (NKJV); Psalm 115:16 (NKJV)

church's holistic role in society should reflect that.

When God is referring to his own glory in Exodus 33, he defines it as his goodness, mercy and compassion.[140] We bring God glory when we practically work out his love into his world. I have previously discussed the implications of Isaiah 58. God's priority for people's well-being over religious rites is clear from this passage. When Jesus introduces his earth mission as the fulfilment of Isaiah 61, again we see its holistic nature.[141] As Christ's body which continues the work of Christ on earth, the church will reflect the breadth of mission he had. Indeed, this breadth will be what separates the sheep from the goats at the final judgement. The sheep welcomed into the future kingdom, will be those who have demonstrated God's love to the hungry, vulnerable, sick and victims of injustice.[142]

The salt of the earth is no good contained in a salt cellar and the light of the world should not be hid under a bowl.[143] The word used by Matthew for world in this reference is 'Kosmos' which is not just the earth or a geographical area or the people of a place. It means the social infrastructure that helps communities function in an orderly way.

Every society has seven aspects: family, religion, business, education,

---

[140] Exodus 33:18,19 (NKJV)
[141] Luke 4:18-19 (NKJV)
[142] Matthew 25:31-46 (NKJV)
[143] Matthew 5:13-16 (NKJV)

government, arts and media. The church has been reasonably good at serving the first two, but not the last five. The last five could be described as the market place. Generalising, there has been reluctance for the church to engage with the market-place for fear of compromising its faith. Instead of being a bright light for the darkening culture, the church, hidden in its own sub-culture, has concealed the light.

Another pivotal passage is Jesus' encounter with the expert in the law.[144] Springing from this we find a summary of the whole Bible, love God and love people, and a famous parable to illustrate the importance of being 'good Samaritans' in our world.

Paul's beautiful passage on the essential nature of love in Corinthians[145] provides teaching on the very foundation of all that may be done in the name of Christ to make a difference in our world. Galatians 5:6 and 1 John 4:21 are two more of many other verses that indicate the importance of love in all we do.

The 'loving God, loving people' theme has become very important to me and provided some sermon material that, together with the work of the Holy Spirit, has deeply affected many hearts. Understanding the unconditional nature of God's love to the people around us will significantly transition our hearts towards them.

---

[144] Luke 10:25-37 (NKJV)
[145] 1 Cor 13 (NKJV)

Principles from Nehemiah:

Principles for leading a church through a season of change can be clearly seen when studying the book of Nehemiah. To help a church to put into practice these principles, a practical study could be worked through with the following points. I have included some quotes from Dan Southerland's book, 'Transitioning', to illustrate the steps further.

Step 1: Preparing for Vision:

"Vision is not just the finish line, it is the whole race". [146] Before a church can receive God's vision we must prepare for it. Nehemiah spent time collecting information about the situation in Jerusalem (Neh. 1:1-2). As he began to understand the situation, he developed a righteous discontent with it (Neh. 1:4).

The church needs to be concerned enough to be motivated into a right response. The right expression of motivated people is to purposefully pray and seek God (Neh. 1:5-6).

The first key from this study reveals that right preparation results in well formed, clear vision.

Step 2: Defining the Vision:

"The three steps to defining vision are: discover your purpose, define your target and decide your strategy"?[147] During a three month period, Nehemiah prayed and vision formed (Neh. 1:4). Out of a prolonged

---

[146] Dan Southerland, *Transitioning*, Grand Rapids: Zondervan (2002), p21
[147] Dan Southerland, *Transitioning*, Grand Rapids: Zondervan (2002), p45

season of prayer a church can reaffirm its purpose, discover its mission and define its strategy.

There is a second key here: the more specific the vision, the more dynamic the results.

Step 3: Planting the Vision:

"Vision is a living seed that must be planted in the proper soil".[148]

The next step is to secure the approval of the key people. Nehemiah secured the king's approval (Neh. 2:5-9). Then secure the assistance of those whose help will be needed and seek the advice and counsel of the leadership team. The team should be built carefully for the purpose of fulfilling the vision (Neh. 2:12).

It is wise to work quietly behind the scenes to begin with (Neh. 2:17) and survey the current situation (Neh. 2:13).

A key to planting the vision, could be to expose key leaders to model churches.

Step 4: Sharing the Vision:

Vision must be effectively communicated to the church and there are

---

[148] Dan Southerland, *Transitioning*, Grand Rapids: Zondervan (2002), p67

many ways to share it. Vision can also be shared outside the church with community and local government. To partner with local government in order to see vision accomplished is to follow in Nehemiah's footsteps (Neh. 2:7-8).

The key for this step would be to understand that vision is both taught and caught; it must be shared in many ways.

Step 5: Implementing the vision:

Implement the changes needed in a strategic order (Neh. 3:1-32). This may involve putting key leaders to work in a visible place (Neh. 3:1-32) and empowering others to work where they are vested (Neh. 3:1-32).

The fifth key is to build on strengths, not on weaknesses.

Step 6: Dealing with opposition:

"Don't let the complainers set the agenda of your church".[149] It is crucial for survival to know what opposition to expect and how to stay on track (Neh. 4).

Therefore the sixth key is: do not take criticism personally, but learn to manage it and keep on task.

---

[149] Dan Southerland, *Transitioning*, Grand Rapids: Zondervan, (2002), p125

Step 7: Making Course Corrections:

"The only thing more painful than learning from experience is not learning from experience!"[150]

Some adjustments will need to be made as the church progresses towards the vision.

In Nehemiah's case, he needed to care for the neglected (Neh. 5:7b). When there are issues to deal with, we need to take action, negotiate peace and stay among the people (Neh. 5:14-18).

The key to go with this step: continually remind the people why you are changing.

Step 8: Evaluating the Results:

"If you build vision, God will send you the leaders you need to accomplish that vision."[151]

There will be evidence that the vision is accomplished (Neh. 6:15). Accomplishment of vision goals will be a great encouragement and a measure of the vision making progress. Such progress provides a clear demonstration of God's work (Neh. 6:16) and God's favour on the

---

[150] Dan Southerland, *Transitioning*, Grand Rapids: Zondervan (2002), p130
[151] Dan Southerland, *Transitioning*, Grand Rapids: Zondervan (2002), p154

work has a great effect on the people.

Nehemiah experienced continued opposition and criticism (Neh. 6:19) and churches have to realise that negative elements will always accompany vision.

There are other major points about transition we can learn from Nehemiah. For example, when progressing towards clear vision there will be opportunity for the emergence of new leaders (Neh. 7:1); there will be major contributions by the people (Neh. 12:47, 13:12); money will flow toward vision (Neh. 12,13); new people will be drawn to the vision and want to be involved in it (Neh. 11:1); and there will be an openness to further change.

Lessons from Joshua

Another rich source of material is a study of the early chapters of the Book of Joshua. The lessons of transition from Joshua can be used to help the church understand where it is going with a series of 'from to' sermons: from wilderness to promise; from wandering to purpose; from maintenance to battle; from audience to army; from settlers to pioneers; from tent dwellers to city takers; from reliance to reliability. Everything was different on the other side of the Jordan: vision, leadership, God's provision, the miracles, purpose, structure, strategy. Everything changed. Everyone was involved. Teaching biblically into transition helps many people come to terms with the need for change, although there will be those who decide that the changes being proposed are too radical.

Appendix 2

Detailed list of service provision at BCLC after transition. (This is a snapshot of provision before I left.)

Oasis Coffee Bar – Open daily to the public from 10am to 3pm. Opportunities for volunteering in serving, food preparation and cleaning duties

Fitness4All Family Fitness Centre – Open daily (70 hours / week). Fitness programmes designed for all ages and all levels of fitness. Qualified instructors. Opportunities for volunteering at reception and cleaning duties.

Opening Hours:

Monday to Friday – 8am to 7pm

Saturday - 9am to 12noon

Multi-Purpose Main Hall – 4 A Side Football League, Karate, Badminton, Netball, Basketball, Line Dancing, Conferences, Exhibitions, Concerts, Band Practice, Church Services, Children & Youth programmes.

Programme:

Monday – Excel Sports 10.30 to 11.30 (youth and adults with disabilities)

       - Rock Kids Club – 5pm to 7pm

- Rock Youth Club – 7.30pm to 9pm (school years 5-7)

Tuesday – Zone Youth Club – 5.30pm to 7pm (school year 5+)

- Youth Club – 7.30pm to 9pm (school years 8-10)

Wednesday – Youth Chess Club 5.45pm to 6.30pm (school year 5+)

- Youth Guitar Lessons 5pm to 5.45pm (school year 5+)

- Excel Sports 6pm to 7pm (youth and adults with disabilities)

- Men's Football - 7.30 to 8.45

Thursday – Advance Line Dancing – 8pm to 10.30pm

Sunday – See church programme,

- Ladies Netball – 6pm to 8pm

Excel Sports – Sport and exercise sessions for young people and adults with disabilities – two sessions weekly (one day session/one evening session).

Programme:

Monday – 10.30am to 11.30am (youth and adults with disabilities)

Wednesday – 6pm – 7pm

Wheelchair Football – weekly session starting shortly

Tennis Courts – Two tennis courts are available to the public for use during the spring and summer months (by arrangement)

Toddlers – Parents and toddler group (two sessions weekly).

Programme:

Thursday – 10am to 12am (English)

Friday – 10am – 12am (Welsh)

Children – Children's clubs (two sessions weekly), BCBC Play Scheme facilitation, Summer Clubs.

Programme:

Monday – 10am to 12noon (nursery to year 4) – summer club

Tuesday - 10am to 12noon (nursery to year 4) – summer club

Wednesday - 10am to 12noon (nursery to year 4) – summer club

Youth – Young people's clubs (3 sessions weekly), Guitar Lessons, Chess Club, Summer Holiday Camp for 11-16 years.

Programme:

Monday – 1pm to 5pm - Summer Club - school years 5 to 7

Tuesday – 1pm to 5pm – Summer Club - school years 8 to 6th form

Tuesday – 7pm to 9pm – 'Oasis' (life from a different angle)

Wednesday - 1pm to 5pm - Summer Club - school years 5 to 7

Thursday - 1pm to 5pm – Summer Club - school years 8 to 6th form

Friday – Trips - 10am to 6pm

        Youth Alpha Course – 7pm to 9pm

Youth Work Course – OCN Level 2 – accredited

Sunday clubs for Créche, Children and Youth.

Programme:

Busy Bees – 10.45am to 12noon (Babies 0-3)

Champs Club – 10.45am to 12noon (4-8years)

Rock Sunday – 10.45 to 12noon (9-11years)

Toasters – 10.45 to 12noon (12-18years)

Counselling – Counselling service available to the public – **by appointment only** – specialist counselling for Cognitive Behavioural Therapy and Schema Therapy, Counselling for Survivors of Sexual Abuse, Drug and Alcohol Counselling, Suicide Counselling, Personality Disorder Therapy, Referral Assessment for Counselling and Therapy, Drug and Alcohol Awareness Courses, Suicide Awareness Course, Basic Counselling Courses (OCN Accredited), Mentoring, Parenting Courses, Debt and Money Management Advice, Skills for Life Courses.

Programme:

Counselling sessions by qualified counsellors – Monday to Thursday (by appointment)

Counselling Course 1 – OCN Level 2 part 1 – accredited

Counselling Course 2 – OCN Level 2 part 2 – accredited

Counselling Course 3 – OCN Level 3 – accredited

Community Connections Project – Recycling of Furniture & Clothes, Food Store project operating from a rented industrial unit. Help in the Community Project - Sick and shut-in visiting and sitting, collecting shopping, take messages, provide transport to doctors and hospital appointments and providing visits and company. Help given to homeless people and people who are or have been drug or alcohol dependant. Such people helped into secure housing, providing support to obtain correct grants and allowances from statutory and other authorities. Volunteers provide respite support for children who are in care - helping the carers to have an occasional break. Christmas Hampers Project. Many volunteering opportunities from reception to furniture repair and clothes cleaning, ironing and packaging, van driving for delivery of furniture, food and clothes, sales assistants, visitors, shopping assistants etc. Social Services Family Reunion facilities, Fruit & Flowers project to help support bereaved and sick people/families.

Adult Education Courses – Stitch craft, Jewellery, Computers (3 sessions), Digital Photography, Languages (Welsh, French & Spanish), Youth Leader courses (OCN accredited). (There is a partnership with WEA and YMCA College to help deliver the adult education programme), Student and undergraduate placements.

Programme:

Monday – Creative Stitch-craft – 10am to 12noon

Tuesday – Introduction to IT – 10am to 12am

     - Family History – 12.30 to 2.30pm

     - Digilab – 3.30pm to 5.30pm

Wednesday – Fabric Painting - 10am to 12noon

Thursday – Using the Internet - 1pm to 3pm

- Digital Photography – 5pm to 7pm

Friday – Spanish for Beginners – 10am to 12noon

- French for Beginners – 12.30pm to 2.30pm

Dorcus Group - Christmas Shoe Box project, food and clothes parcels for poor families, clothes for Eastern Europe project, knitting, friendship. – Volunteers and new members welcome

Programme:

Wednesday: 2pm to 4pm

Modern Relevant Church – Christian worship service – Sunday 1030 to 1230.

Weekly courses - Alpha courses, Understanding Christianity courses, Understanding your SHAPE courses-understanding what your gifts and talents are and encouragement to serve in the community. Weddings, funerals and child dedications conducted. Pastoral care of church attendees and community, Small Group meetings for friendship and Christian teaching, A part time church consultant was also employed helping advise church communities in Wales to be more community focussed. Volunteering opportunities for setting up/down and cleaning.

Programme:

Morning Service – 10.30am to 12.00noon

Evening Service – 6.30pm to 8pm (fortnightly)

DigiLab – Fully equipped computer and digital equipment Centre primarily for 16 – 25 year olds but open to all ages. Wireless internet facility, Training Room facility.

Programme:

Tuesday – 3.30pm to 5.30pm (and also by appointment)

Mini Bus – The 'Extra Mile' Mini Bus with disabled access facility is available to transport people to Centre activities (by arrangement).

Facilities for Conferencing, Meetings, Catering – conferencing and meeting are fully catered for up to 300 people. Fully equipped rooms, excellent communication facilities

Wedding parties – Catering facilities for wedding parties of up to 150 people

Parties – Children's parties, football parties.

Schools – BCLC provide qualified personnel to help in the local schools – After school clubs, fitness and healthy eating programmes, Assemblies.

BCLC also contracted to supply various facilities and training during the week to 24 young people who are not attending school and for whom an alternative curriculum has been arranged.

Overseas Projects – BCLC sponsor Christian organisations in Poland, Uruguay and Brazil who have similar social and community ethos and programmes.

In Brazil BCLC fully sponsors 30 pupils in a school in Patos, NE Brazil.

Appendix 3

Outcome Stories

There were so many lives that were transformed during and after transition. Each story is precious to God and to the church. I have highlighted just a few below and changed all names to maintain confidentiality.

Pete came from London to live with his grandparents who were members of BCLC. Pete was a drug addict, gambler and became caught up in the violent lifestyle of some on the Isle of Dogs. He had become unemployable because of his habit and a constant worry for his parents. Pete started to come to church at BCLC and soon found his life changing. He was saved, freed of his addictions, and employed part-time with the LEA in a school and part-time at BCLC as a youth worker.

Sally had been coming to BCLC for many years. Recently made redundant, Sally became depressed and found the redundancy difficult to cope with. There were financial pressures resulting. Sally began to volunteer at BCLC and through counselling found herself in a better place.

Elaine had a very dysfunctional and abused background and as a result had serious mental health issues. Elaine worked with mental health professionals, our own counsellors and others at BCLC providing support. She became much improved and volunteered two days a week at BCLC.

Sport and fitness stories

Ralph was recovering from a stroke he suffered. He visited the gym twice weekly and made good steady progress.

Maurene was registered blind, but enjoyed the safe environment of the gym and the humour!

Joan was recovering from brain cancer but enjoyed being active again as she had personal supervision within the gym.

Mike had just been released from hospital with bipolar depression and alcoholism. Coming to the gym was part of his integration into normal life after hospital.

Phil was fifty one. Deteriorating health and obesity brought Phil to the gym. Under supervision Phil changed his diet and with regularly exercise, lost a stone in weight.

The gym was also used by the under 16 Bridgend rugby team, the local cadet group doing a sponsored run, young people from the local schools, day centres looking after the disabled and many working people taking advantage of the early morning openings and evening sessions.

Youth Story

"Gary had been bullied for a year in school before he made his parents aware of it. When they found out, they contacted me so that we as a youth team could be aware of it. We noticed that Gary was much quieter than normal, to the point where he was saying that he had gone off football – the love of his life. One of our volunteers got talking to him and he admitted feelings of suicide. I was then brought into the situation and ended up taking him home and talking with his mother. She explained that Gary wanted to move schools to get away from the bullies, but she was concerned that the bulling may continue in the new school. A meeting was set up with the Deputy Head of his school, his Head of Year, his mother and me as his Youth Leader. Gary did decide to move schools, but through the support of all parties, the transition went well and Gary has returned to his normal self and of course the love of his life, football." (Youth Manager)

Disabled sports story

"Jill lives with Cerebral Palsy. We first met her three years ago when she came to a taster session we put on for a multi-sports session we were considering running on a weekly basis for adults with disabilities. Jill did not do anything without her carer, who would walk with her arm in arm wherever they went. Her carer would pick the ball up for her, throw the ball for her and do most of the things for her that Jill struggled to do herself. Three years on, we now run two weekly multi-sports sessions that are attended by Jill. Her mother drops her off without a carer, she can play all the sports that we play and rarely requires one to one attention. She progressed so much that she won our first ever 'Most Improved Player Award' in the Spring." (Sports Coordinator)

Counselling Stories

"Bill came to the session presenting O.C.D., his marriage was affected and he had broken sleep patterns. It had developed into a fear of answering the telephone which was an extra stress as he worked on a telephone help line at an employment centre. He was in therapy for six weeks working on his schemas and completing a daily thoughts/feelings diary. He was able to resist checking all secure places three times and he felt confident in using the telephone.

Rob was a high risk suicide. We worked with depression and now he is doing well at University.

Sara was a persistent self harmer. We worked with schema's and evidence of thoughts of guilt. She is still in therapy but in six months has only self harmed three times despite having had two traumatic events in her life during this period.

Chris was a young man with anger issues and because of lack of control he would use alcohol to extreme. We worked with reasons for anger, which helped him to deal with the thoughts that raised his anger level. In the first three weeks he stopped drinking and was able to identify the hot spots in anger and control them. He is still doing very well."

(Therapist)

Centre story

"I saw the Coffee shop sign whilst driving through Cefn Cribwr one day and decided to call in. After a delicious lunch we began to chat with the ladies. Somehow or other, before I left the Coffee shop, I had volunteered my services as a cook one day a week.

Twelve months have passed, and I eagerly look forward to my weekly challenge of providing home cooked favourites for the Coffee shop.

A chance visit has paid dividends, I get to do something I really enjoy and at the same time, am able to contribute to this worthwhile organisation." (Jacky)

Bibliography

Barna George, *Turnaround Churches*, California: Regal Books (1993)

Beckham William, *The Second Reformation*, Houston: Touch Outreach Ministries (1995)

Boucher Daniel, *Taking our place. Church in the community*, Cardiff: Gweini (2002)

Crow Iain, France Alan, Hacking Sue, and Hart Mary *Does Communities that Care work? An evaluation of a community-based risk prevention programme in three neighbourhoods*, York: Joseph Rowntree Foundation (2004)

Dan Southerland, *Transitioning*, Grand Rapids: Zondervan (2002)

Evans John M., *Faith in Wales: Counting for communities*, Cardiff: Gweini (2008)

Frost Michael & Hirsch Alan, *The shaping of things to come: Innovation and Mission for the 21st Century Church,* (Massachusetts: Hendrickson, 2003)

Gibbs Eddie & Coffey Ian, *Church Next*, Nottingham: IVP (2001)

Goleman Daniel, Boyatziz Richard & McKee Annie, *The New Leaders: Transforming the Art of Leadership into the Science of Results*, Boston: Little Brown/Havard Business School Press (2002)

Goss Steve, *Freedom in Christ Discipleship Course*, Reading: FICM UK (2006)

Greenleaf Robert K., *Servant Leadership*, New Jersey: Paulist Press (2002)

Greenslade Philip, *Leadership*, Basingstoke: Marshalls Paperbacks (1984)

Hammer Michael, *Beyond Reengineering*, New York: Harper Collins, (1996)

Herrington Jim, Bonem Mike & Furr James, *Leading Congregational Change; Workbook: A practical Guide for the Transformational Journey*, Dallas: Jossy-Bass (2000)

Herrington Jim, Bonem Mike & Furr James, *Leading Congregational Change; A practical Guide for the Transformational Journey*, Dallas: Jossy-Bass (2000)

Huggett J., *Listening to God*, London: Hodder & Stroughton (1986)

Hybels Bill, *The Volunteer Revolution: Unleashing the Power of Everybody* Grand Rapids: Zondervan (2004)

Malphurs Aubrey, *Planting Growing churches*, Grand Rapids: Baker Books (1998)

Mann Alice, *Can our church live?: Redeveloping congregations in decline*, Bethesda, Md.: Alban Institute (1999)

Marshall Tom, *Understanding Leadership*, Tonbridge: Sovereign World (1991)

McLaren Brian D, *The Church on the other Side*, Grand Rapids: Zondervan (2000)

McManus Erwin, *An Unstoppable Force*, Orange: Group Publishing (2001)

Robinson & Smith, *Invading Secular Space*, London: Monarch Books (2003)

Roxburgh & Romanuk, *The Missional Leader*, San Fransisco: Jossey-Bass (2006)

Roxburgh Alan, *The Sky is falling: Leaders lost in transition*, Eagle: Allelon Press (2006)

Samuel Vinay & Sugden Chris, *Mission as Transformation*, Oxford: Regnum Books (1999)

Stott John, *New Issues Facing Christians Today*, Grand Rapids: Zondervan (1999)

The Holy Bible, Nashville: Thomas Nelson (1982)

Wagner Peter C., *The New Apostolic Churches*, Ventura: Regal Books (1998)

Wheatley Margaret, *Leadership and the New Science*, San Fransisco: Berret-Koehler (2006)

TIM Course Notes

Module 406.1, *Mission History,* Together in Mission

Module 406.1 *The Nature and Purpose of Church,* Together in Mission

Module 406.3 *The Management and Culture of Change,* Together in Mission

Module 406.4 *Mission and Empowerment,* Together in Mission

Module 406.5 *From Vision to Reality,* Together in Mission

Websites:

Clarke Dr Peter, *Understanding an integral mission approach.* www.viva.org (Jan. 2007)

Evangelical Action Brazil, www.eabrazil.com

Malphurs Aubrey, *Advanced Strategic Planning Method*, www.malphursgroup.com (Dec. 2009)

Mead Margaret (1901-1978) www.interculturalstudies.org (Dec 2009)

Rick Warren's Second Reformation. Interview with David Kuo. www.beliefnet.com (Dec 2009)

The Alban Institute, www.holyconversations.org (Dec. 2009)

The Teal Trust, www.teal.org.uk (Dec. 2009)

Warren Rick, Class 301, www.pastors.com (Dec. 2009)

Welsh Index of Multiple Deprivation 2005: Local Authority Analysis – Bridgend, www.wales.gov.uk (April 2010)

www.cwvys.org.uk/en/docs/Youth_Work_Curriculum_Statement_for_Wales_English.pdf (Dec 2009)

Conferences

Porter Michael, *Strategy and Leadership*, The Global leadership Summit 2007, Willow Creek, www.willowcreekglobalsummit.org

Other

Communities that Care unpublished local report (2003)

David Melding AM, 17th December 2002, Speech, The National Assembly for Wales.

Lord Griffiths of Fforestfach, 9th December 2002, IWP Lecture, Aberystwyth.

Janet Ryder AM, for a Cardiff Institute for Contemporary Christianity (CICC) politics interview in 2003.

Jay A. Conger and Rabindra N. Kanungo, *The Empowerment Process: Integrating Theory and Practice,* Briarcliff Manor, NY: The Academy of Management Review, Vol. 13, No. 3 (Jul. 1988)

Printed in Great Britain
by Amazon

82970727R00081